Endorsement of "Free to Be Me"

What a timely book. How many times over 30 years of pastoring do I wish I had a book like this to hand to people I've counselled!

Graham deals with the master emotion of shame from many different angles and reveals how this root which is so often hidden, is the cause of many of the inner struggles we deal with, in ourselves, our relationships, and even our walk with God. The truths are pertinent, the stories are real to life, and the potential for freedom for anyone reading this is... well, exponential!

CRAIG BUROKER
SENIOR PASTOR
SOUTHSIDE VICTORY
CHURCH FELLOWSHIP

Shame can manifest as one limiting factor that keeps people stuck, costs them money and impairs their ability to truly reach their full potential.

I absolutely love the lyrics of the song, "Holy Spirit" written by Bryan and Katie Torwalt. Those words have become creeds and an inspiration to me: "I've tasted and seen of the sweetest of loves Where my heart becomes free and my shame is undone" Till these aspirations are manifest in our heart, we truly are not free.

In *Free To Be Me*, Graham challenges everything we think we know about shame. Based on years of research, teaching and counselling, he argues that shame is not weakness, but rather our clearest path to courage, engagement, vulnerability and meaningful connection to God and others. We are to learn to trade our shame for the joyful freedom that comes from the Lord.

A depletion of personal freedom breeds fear: fear of personal reality and fear of others. When people are depleted of freedom, they cling to illusions, prejudices and lies about themselves and their power to change. Governed by compulsions, they discourage and disparage people. They leave people worse off than when they found them. Under the control of compulsions, others can quickly become a threat: they stand in the way of the love and success we seem to need so badly. It is a liberation from shame that opens us up and leads us to the discovery of our common humanity.

Free To Be Me will enhance the quality of your life, help you undo the work of shame in your life and set you free to show up in ways that are healthy, helpful, and uplifting. It will spark a new spirit of truth—and trust—in churches, families, schools, and communities.

A brilliant piece of work! Graham was able to take an everyday subject and turn it into a compelling read that I have recommended to all of my colleagues. A brilliant piece of work! As a pastor, this is a must read! Free To Be Me will be my go-to-guide for many years to come.

DR. DANIEL ZOPOULA
PRESIDENT, BRIDGES OF HOPE INTERNATIONAL NETWORK
PASTOR, THE MIZ CITY CHURCH
ARCHBISHOP, INTERNATIONAL HOUSE OF THE COMMUNION
OF EVANGELICAL EPISCOPAL CHURCHES

"Free to be Me, Turning Shame into Freedom" is an insightful book that draws from Graham's extensive experience in dealing with those who have felt the sting of failure and rejection caused by shame. I know first hand the feeling of hopelessness and loss caused by failure and shame, but no matter how dark the night, there is joy in the morning. This book will help bring healing to the hurting and insight for those who seek to help others who struggle under the heavy load of shame.

DICK DEWEERT B.TH. D.D.
FOUNDER, PRESIDENT
DOMINION MEDIA
THIRD DAY CHURCH

Having walked with Graham for over thirty years, as a close friend, fellow collogue and companion in ministry, gives me a broad perspective from which to review Graham's latest book. He brings together a blend of insightful intellect and spiritual discernment to the issues of shame and guilt. What he shares is rooted in diligent research, personal experience and thousands of hours of counseling. Your understanding of yourself and intimacy with the Lord will be enriched through reading and applying the truths in this book.

DUANE HARDER – COUNSELLOR AND
SPIRITUAL FATHER TO GRAHAM

In his latest book, *Free to Be Me*, Graham Bretherick provides a comprehensive study of the origins and impact of shame in our lives. Using his own life experiences, and stories gathered from many years as a counselling psychologist, Graham transparently and comprehensively shares about the difference between shame and guilt; negative and positive shame; and, overall, provides practical tools for effectively dealing with shame in our lives – so we can fully walk in God's freedom. I've known Graham for over twenty years, as a counsellor and father figure, and can testify the teachings detailed in this book have been life changing for me and, I'm confident, will be for you also!

IAN BYRD – LEAD PASTOR, CHURCH OF THE ROCK CALGARY;
MEMBER OF THE LEADERSHIP COUNCIL OF
THE LIFELINKS INTERNATIONAL FAMILY OF CHURCHES

Graham presents the difference between guilt and shame and how false guilt can turn into shame, in a clear and understandable manner. His insights, which come from biblical wisdom and decades of real life counselling experience and teaching, will captivate the reader. His wisdom will bring hope and comfort, along with practical ways to overcome the negative effects of our behaviour and the lies we have believed about ourselves. This teaching has impacted the way I as a pastor and parent understand my members, and has equipped me to walk them through the journey of healing and freedom in the areas of guilt and shame.

REV. JEFFREY SMITH,
MISSIONARY TO THE PHILIPPINES.

Graham's and Sherry's God given intrinsic desire to help people forward on life's journey is the earmark of their influence. His initial book on Anger & Forgiveness entitled ~ 'Healing Life's Hurts' and his second ~ ' The Fear

Shift' are the evidences of a life reflecting his heart throb and ministry name: Run Free.

My wife and I recommend his latest book to you on what seems to be the most sinister of life's hidden bondages. Shame reflects itself with Octopi-like tentacles, which seek to choke and suffocate the very life from its prey, this being humankind. Graham's writings are that of a 'theopractor at his work' reflecting a biblical rational theology and applied biblical practice working together to set captives free.

Kenn & Cheryl Gill
Apostolic Leaders
Ripple Effect Ministries
Calgary, Alberta

Although shame has been a part of human experience for thousands of years, most of us do not clearly recognize this emotion, discern its harm or benefit, nor understand the outcomes it produce in ourselves, our families, and our culture. The fact that shame is rarely discussed in society, including in most churches, is all the more reason why books such as Graham Bretherick's "Free to Be Me" need to be written and read. It is also why, without apology, I offer this blanket statement: anyone who wishes their soul to be truly free in this life, or who desires to counsel others to be free, must understand the key concepts presented in this book.

Fortunately, these important ideas are readily accessible; while squarely founded on both the principles of Scripture and modern research, like his first two books on anger and fear, Graham's third book appeals to heart and mind without burdensome psychobabble or esoteric theological terms. Short sections dotted with examples and testimonies make for easy reading, and helpful prayers and challenges for the reader are interspersed throughout. Graham understands how difficult it can be to open up and investigate the sensitive areas of our lives, and he gently encourages readers to go beyond reading *about* shame and actually experience freedom.

Dr. K. D. Bennett
Church Planter and Missionary
Shanghai, China

I believe shame is a topic that can never be discussed enough. From my experience shame limits the expression of who we are and we often don't realize these limitation(s), at least not until we feel bad enough about ourselves. I believe if everyone could appreciate and comprehend the prison that shame creates, they would be frantically exposing their own shame in an effort to get free. Most do not know the bondage they are in. That is the subtlety of shame. It undermines you and you don't even know it. Read this book. Seek to understand yourself. Get free.

DR RANDY JOHNSON
REGISTERED PSYCHOLOGIST
DIRECTOR, MASTER'S COUNSELLING SERVICES
CALGARY ALBERTA

"I have great admiration for my dear friend Graham Bretherick who has regularly come to India and trained our church folks in various aspects of counselling. And I am so glad that he is travelling the world over to do the same. We have been immensely blessed by his training and material in the past and, having read the manuscript of this new book, I am confident it will serve most of us who suffer from guilt and shame. His humility oozes out from the book as he shares tons of his own stories of shame and that will surely put the readers at ease and allow them to open the door to be set free from the prison of shame."

STANLEY MEHTA IS THE EX-OVERSEER OF A GROUP OF CHURCHES CALLED GATEWAY MINISTRIES INTERNATIONAL WHICH HAS PLANTED 120 HOUSE CHURCHES IN INDIA AND ABROAD. HE HAS WRITTEN SEVERAL BOOKS, PLANTED A BIBLE SCHOOL AND STARTED A SOCIAL WORK AMONG THE UNDERPRIVILEGED.

The powerful emotion of shame is used by Satan against us to keep control over our lives. When we carry shame, it affects more than just us. Readers of "Free to be Me" are more than likely to find themselves relating to what Graham writes and ask themselves the question now and again, "I wonder if I have dealt with that in my life?" Don't be surprised when you discover that there are still some areas of shame in your life. This book provides many examples of causes of negative shame in the author's own life and how he was redeemed from it. If you too would like to be "Free to be Me", this book will provide you practical helps to achieve that goal!

BILL ZWARTBOL

PASTOR, FREE GRACE FELLOWSHIP

LETHBRIDGE, AB

FREE TO BE ME

FREE TO BE ME
Turning Shame into Freedom

Graham Bretherick

ELM HILL

A Division of
HarperCollins Christian Publishing

www.elmhillbooks.com

Free to Be Me
Turning Shame into Freedom

Published in Nashville, Tennessee, by Elm Hill, an imprint of Thomas Nelson. Elm Hill and Thomas Nelson are registered trademarks of HarperCollins Christian Publishing, Inc.

Elm Hill titles may be purchased in bulk for educational, business, fund-raising, or sales promotional use. For information, please e-mail SpecialMarkets@ ThomasNelson.com.

Scripture quotations marked NIV are from the Holy Bible, New International Version˙, NIV˙. Copyright © 1973, 1978, 1984, 2011 by Biblica, Inc.˙ Used by permission of Zondervan. All rights reserved worldwide. www.Zondervan.com. The "NIV" and "New International Version" are trademarks registered in the United States Patent and Trademark Office by Biblica, Inc.˙

Scripture quotations marked NASB are from New American Standard Bible˙. Copyright © 1960, 1962, 1963, 1968, 1971, 1972, 1973, 1975, 1977, 1995 by The Lockman Foundation. Used by permission. (www.Lockman.org)

Library of Congress Cataloging-in-Publication Data

Library of Congress Control Number: 2018955202

ISBN 978-1-595559050 (Paperback)
ISBN 978-1-595558824 (Hardbound)
ISBN 978-1-595558954 (Ebook)

FOREWORD

It's with great honour that we scribe this foreword to Graham's most recent book.

Graham's and Sherry's God-given intrinsic desire to help people forward on life's journey is the earmark of their influence. His initial book on anger and forgiveness entitled *Healing Life's Hurts* and his second, *The Fear Shift*, are evidences of a life reflecting his heartthrob and ministry name: *Run Free*.

Free to Be Me is the trilogy title of this book. All three books stem from a lifetime of hands-on experience, data gathering, and insights on pertinent subjects that enslave men and women ensnared by emotional and spiritual bondages. Over a decade ago I asked Graham if he would assist us in giving birth to a newly forming leadership network. My wife and I asked him firstly if he would begin with us as a core group in a series of encounters entitled a 'Journey to Emotional Health and a Vibrant Spirituality.' This he did. He has since travelled throughout the network and beyond doing the same. Why this course of action? We believe that one cannot fully enjoy the vibrancy of our spirituality without true emotional health. His three writings point directly towards freeing people from anger by applied forgiveness, being freed from fear, by embraced and applied love, and now freedom from the concealed nature of shame through applied humility and grace from God.

My wife and I recommend his latest book to you on what seems to be the most sinister of life's hidden bondages. Shame reflects itself with octopuslike tentacles, which seek to choke and suffocate the very life from its prey, this being humankind. Graham's writings are that of a 'theopractor at his work' reflecting a biblical rational theology and applied biblical practice working together to set captives free.

Graham invites everyone from behind the 'doors of shame' to the place of embracing the grace of God that frees anyone who welcomes this grace to heal, to liberate, and become the person our Creator designed us to be. This book is an invitation to 'come out of our hiddenness' into full view of our Heavenly Father's acceptance by allowing His heart and His grace to overwhelm us with complete freedom reflecting His nature ~ as declared by His son, 'whom the Son sets free, is free indeed.'

The Passion Translation of the scripture summarizes the subject of freedom and liberty this way in Galations 5:1 ' *Let me be clear, the Anointed One has set us free~not partially, but completely and wonderfully free! We must always cherish this truth and stubbornly refuse to go back into the bondage of our past.*'

May the truth unveiled in this book be mingled together with the power of story and the wisdom of applied grace become like a cord of three strands tied tightly together, enabling us to walk in the light and the lightness of our newfound freedoms. BE FREE!

Kenn and Cheryl Gill
Apostolic Leaders
Ripple Effect Ministries
Calgary, Alberta

PREFACE

Of my three books, this is the most personal of them all. I specifically chose to be more vulnerable in writing this book because I have discovered, through my workshops on shame, that my vulnerability invites others to be vulnerable. I wrestled with shame for many years but I did not realize it. When I was developing my workshop on shame years ago, I struggled to acknowledge my "shame demons" and, as a result, it took me two extra years to get the workshop completed. I am grateful, however, that God put the desire to experience true freedom in my life and He gave me the grace to push through and finish this book.

I have a sense that the enemy did not want me to complete this book. When the manuscript was about halfway finished, I experienced a computer glitch and lost most of the material. I was in the Philippines at the time and my laptop computer started acting up at my hotel. I had never had any problems before on this laptop (I do acknowledge that I didn't have the manuscript adequately backed up). I tried to recover the manuscript material in the Philippines to no avail. Back in Canada my friend Steve who is a computer whiz also attempted unsuccessfully to recover the lost work (to his chagrin). When he could not recover my manuscript, he recommended an expert in data recovery in Lethbridge and even this person could not find the lost material.

Initially, I was overwhelmed with the loss. However, once God revealed to me that this was enemy attack, the choice to push through the difficulty and fight back became all too clear. I diligently rewrote all the lost material. I refused to let the enemy keep this book from being published. I sensed that God was testing my heart to see if I would persevere in getting the book published. To my knowledge, there are very few books currently in print that deal with the subject of shame from a Christian perspective. Knowing this motivated me even further to press on and finish my writing

My main purpose for writing this book is to help people find freedom from their shame. Shame is the most misunderstood of all the emotions. In psychology, shame is called the "sleeper" emotion, because most of us are so unaware of its effect in our lives. Naturally, we can't find freedom from shame until we realize the overwhelming hold that it has in our lives. I love it when I see people dealing with their shame because shame robs them of the power of God and steals their God-given destiny.

As you walk with me through this journey to understand shame and guilt, I am praying that you will find the same freedom that I have found in my life. I love my freedom in Christ. Galatians 5:1 tells us, "It is for freedom that Christ has set us free. Stand firm, then, and do not let yourselves be burdened again by a yoke of slavery." As you read this book, I trust that God's words through me will guide you on your own journey to freedom.

ACKNOWLEDGEMENTS

I have so much for which to be thankful in my life. That makes it challenging to write a relatively concise list of acknowledgments because countless people have contributed to my life, out of which comes this writing. In my previous books (*Healing Life's Hurts* and *The Fear Shift*) I acknowledged that multitudes of people have built into my life but I want to focus this time on those in particular who have helped me work through my shame issues.

The first of these people would be my wife, Sherry. She has seen me at my best and my worst and still loves me, accepts me, and helps me be honest with myself. My debt of gratitude is immeasurable. I feel as secure as anyone could ever feel in a marriage because of Sherry's unconditional love for me. I am a truly blessed man! I cannot thank her enough. Her help in reading the manuscript (twice) has made the quality of this book significantly better. I am truly grateful.

I am also thankful to Bill Axtell for his editing work. He is hard on my ego but the quality of his editing in all three of my books makes them so much more readable. Because I have taught this material in workshop format for many years, I have a tendency to write like I talk. Bill says that's not a good idea. He has helped me to write with greater clarity and sharpness. I am really appreciative of his editing skill. Karen Alm, our good friend for many years, has crafted the cover of the book, and as always, used her God-given creativity to develop an eye-catching cover which draws people to the inside of the book. Thanks, Karen!

Family is everything to me. My children (Sam, Sarah, Andy, Nathan, and Caleb), their spouses (Lisa, Graham, Sue, and Katie) and my grandchildren (all eleven of them, so far) have also seen me at my best and worst and yet they honour, accept, and affirm me in so many ways. Although they have suffered under my fathering failures (I have also had lots of successes), they have forgiven me countless times and I am indebted.

My parents (Ralph and Marjorie—long since enjoying God's presence) my siblings (Judy, Grant, Ross, Lynne, and Elaine and their spouses, Dan, Lois, Elaine, John, and Jim), Sherry's parents (Alvin, also with the Lord, and Ileana), Sherry's siblings (Lorraine, Chuck, Geoff, and Jeanelle and their spouses, Jon, Marci, and Vance) have all found it in their hearts to see past my weaknesses and accept me and love me. Their love has, and is, one of the greatest means of removing shame barriers in my life. Sometimes, we take our families for granted because we have lived with them in family settings for long periods of time, but I appreciate that they still express their love and affirmation of me.

My spiritual parents, Duane and Marva Harder, and my many colleagues in the faith have contributed much to my spiritual growth and emotional development. I have often said I don't know where I would be today without their direction, correction, and love. I also owe a debt of gratitude to Kenn and Cheryl Gill because they believed in me (and Sherry), and have sent us out to many of their churches to minister freedom to them. My own church family (Pastor Bill Zwartbol and his wife, Elaine, plus my fellow Elders, Neil and Margaret Slingerland

and Bert and Carolin Van Hierden) have also graciously drawn me into relationship and allowed me to be myself in their midst. I am truly grateful.

My Run Free Ministries Board has served me faithfully over many years. Grant Bretherick (yes, my twin brother), Alvin Fritz, David Harrison, Cory Hunt, Peter Van Hierden, and Bill Zwartbol have been an encouragement to me. I've kept them on their toes as they've tried to keep me on track in the call of God in my life. I truly value their love, their support, and their belief in me over many years.

Lastly, I will be forever grateful to Jesus for His Spirit's work in transforming me from an insecure, self-focused, self-determined man into one who has found wonderful security in Father God's love and acceptance. I love living in freedom and I love helping people find that same freedom in Jesus. Moving from a life of shame to a life of freedom is the call that Jesus has given me (and also Sherry). So we are delighted whenever we see others finding freedom in Christ.

Introduction

A story I read years ago concerned two brothers living in China. The younger brother wanted to marry but had no money for the wedding. He asked his older brother to lend him money for his wedding. His brother agreed so the younger brother went ahead with plans for the marriage. Later, when the younger brother was at work, he found a blank cheque belonging to the company. He fell into temptation by writing a cheque to pay back his older brother. Eventually discovered, he was charged with embezzling funds from the company. In China, this was viewed as serious crime. As a result, the younger brother was imprisoned and sentenced to death.

The older brother, distraught, sought advice from a friend, who happened to be a Christian. He asked what he could do to save his younger brother. Through discussion, the friend led him into a relationship with Jesus Christ. The older brother then visited his younger brother in prison. In telling him about Jesus, the older brother realized he needed to write out some information for him. Finding only toilet paper, he used it to explain how to become a Christian.

Consequently, as a new Christian, the younger brother began preaching in the prison. As he preached the Holy Spirit moved significantly, bringing hundreds of inmates to know the Lord Jesus. In the meantime, the older brother connected with some Christians who prayed that God would reduce the younger brother's sentence. God performed a miracle as they prayed. The younger brother's sentence was not only reduced from a death sentence but he also was given probation, an act unheard of in the Chinese justice system of the time. When the younger brother was released from prison the brothers opened a house church, with a specific ministry of praying for release for other prisoners as well as a ministry to prisoners.

God Redeems Shame

Amazingly God can redeem a shameful act and, through redemption, enable people to discover the destiny for which they have been created. The younger brother was not only freed from prison, but he was also freed from a prison of shame. All of us want to live in freedom, especially the freedom that Jesus Christ purchased for us on the cross. But many people do not know how to find the freedom they so want.

God has a plan and purpose for every human. All of us need to find the purpose for which God has created us. No one wants to live a life of restriction because of their past. Although God has a track for us to follow, often our sins, failures, mistakes, hurt, and pain get us sidetracked from God's purpose for our lives. We don't know how to deal with these negative issues so we bury or repress them.

Sometimes, the negative circumstances that happen are extremely painful. At other times, we are either too young or inexperienced to know how to deal with them. With regard to emotional baggage, there are two general issues we tend to repress. The first are offenses that attack us. Our natural response both to offense and hurt is anger. Anger is the psychological mechanism that God, Himself, put in us for protection from danger. However, repressed anger is highly dangerous to us.

The second negative issue that we deal with are the offenses that we cause against other people, called guilt. When we have wronged someone and not dealt with it properly through forgiveness, repentance, and restitution, the offense will transfer into the "shame closet." When guilt issues are not dealt with effectively, they will eventually cause shame.

Guilt arises from behaviour, whereas shame corresponds with identity. When we fail to deal with our shame properly, we will lack freedom in those areas of our lives. Bitterness will reroute into shame; shame will keep us enslaved. This book will help you open the closed doors in your life. God wants all of us free to be the person He created us for, without the impediments of bitterness, anxiety, unresolved guilt, or shame.

God's will is to take the evil done to us, or that we have done to others, and turn it into something positive. He works through the processes of confession and forgiveness with the assistance of the Holy Spirit. He heals areas of pain in amazing ways, working them out both for our good and the good of others. This is the message of Romans 8:28: "And we know that God causes all things to work together for good to those who love God, to those who are called according to His purpose." (NASB) When the Holy Spirit used the word "all," He meant all. God can take our most difficult circumstances and turn them around for good. That is why the gospel is called "good news."

PART 1

INTRODUCING THE CONCEPT OF SHAME

CHAPTER 1

IDENTIFYING WITH SHAME

Shame is an emotion we seldom consider. However, its effect on our lives is far more impacting than most of us realize. In psychology, shame is called the "sleeper" emotion, because we are so unaware of its effect in our lives. Shame functions in us without conscious awareness. The challenge in writing about shame is how to make it interesting enough to capture people's attention so they will read about it. Yet everyone needs this information about shame.

Initially when I first developed this teaching on shame into a workshop, I called it—what else?—"The Shame Workshop." But as I found out, people didn't want to come to a workshop that they considered irrelevant. A pastor friend of mine suggested that what I was really teaching about was freedom from shame, not shame. So I changed the name of the workshop to "Free To Be Me," also the title of this book.

To find freedom, we need to address four major areas in counselling. We need freedom from bitterness, freedom from fear, from guilt, and from shame. Through teaching these subjects over many years, I see confusion comparing guilt feelings to shame. Although many think these emotions are the same, they are not; they are quite distinct from each other.

Interestingly, we are often ashamed of our shame. That is why we repress or bury our shame. We all have shame issues, many of which we don't realize. A core purpose of this book is to give understanding to the hidden issues of shame. However, the main purpose of this book is helping people find freedom. We can't find freedom from shame until we realize shame is a problem.

Shame Affects Us All

Shame affects all of us significantly. That is why I write and teach about this subject. In fact, as I was first developing the workshop on shame, I bumped into my own issues of shame that I had effectively hidden for many years. As I was preparing for the workshop, I put off the work because it was stirring my own "shame demons." God was drawing my attention to the power shame held over my life. I had to resolve my shame concerns before I effectively could help others deal with their shame.

As with my books on anger and fear, I did not want to write primarily from a psychological perspective. So I searched the Bible first and then brought psychological insights into the discussion afterward. I looked up the words *shame, shameful, shamefully, ashamed,* and others in the Bible. Depending on the English translation one uses, there are somewhere between 185 and 190 references to the word *shame* in the Bible.

Seven different Hebrew words and three different Greek words are translated *shame* in the Scriptures. Through research, I was surprised at how much the Bible says about shame. I not only read the verses where the word shame occurs but I also read the context surrounding the verses. Here is one illustration of where the word *shame* appears: Psalm 25:1–3 (NIV)

1   To you, O Lord, I lift up my soul,

2   in you I trust, O my God.

     Do not let me be put to shame,

     nor let my enemies triumph over me.

3   No one whose hope is in you

     will ever be put to shame,

     but they will be put to shame

     who are treacherous without excuse.

This is a Psalm written by David teaching on prayer. Prayer is the lifting up of your soul to God. It is the expression of your mind, emotions, and will to God, to communicate with Him the desires, needs, and concerns of your heart. David starts by saying, "In you I trust O my God." If you want to pray effectively, you must communicate your trust in Father God. You cannot open up to anyone, be that God or even other people, and be vulnerable with them without trust. You simply can't open to anyone without trust. So if you want to be effective in prayer, you must begin by declaring your trust in Him.

The same is true in our human communication. You can communicate superficially with virtually anyone but before you open your heart, you ask yourself whether you can trust this person with your heart. In counselling, trust is always a major concern. People trust Sherry and me with significant details of their lives. Even unaware, they subconsciously ask: can I trust you with my secrets, with my shame issues, with what is precious to me?

Do I Really Trust God?

Similarly, we can't get personal with God unless we truly trust Him. When asked the question: "Do you really trust God?" and your response is: "Well of course, I trust God; I'm a Christian," bear in mind that trust is fundamental to intimacy with God in prayer. That's why many of our prayers are more religious than real.

In verse 2 of Psalm 25, David says: "Do not let me be put to shame, nor let my enemies triumph over me." Psalm 25 is written in Hebrew poetry. A feature of Hebrew poetry is called parallelism. The first line of the verse expresses a truth and the second line in this poetic form is a commentary or amplification of the first line. So the first thing that David says in this Psalm on prayer is, "Do not let me be put to shame." Why? Because he is opening his heart to God and does not want God to use his openness against him. In other words, "When I open up my heart to you, Father, please don't shame me." David is aware of the power of shame to destroy his life.

And then David comments on how it feels to be put to shame—it is like his enemy triumphing over him. That is exactly what shame is: our "enemy" triumphing over us. As a result we look for a place to hide, because of what our enemy can and will do to us. When we feel ashamed we want to hide from everyone, including our spouses, family, friends, and even God.

David's next expression is more positive: "No one whose hope is in you will ever be put to shame." His commentary follows on the first line: "But they will be put to shame who are treacherous without excuse." The phrase "treacherous without excuse" refers to people who live deceitfully. The key to this process of not living a life of shame is being able to trust God, communicate with Him, and trust that God will always meet you when the enemy tries to shame you in defeat.

We will never be put to shame as long we put our hope in God. Most of us, if not all of us, have unresolved shame, yet our hope lies in putting our trust in God. I will repeat this principle throughout this book: our only hope of protection from shame is that God will redeem us from shame. I want to proclaim emphatically: only hope in God heals, restores, and turns our shame into something good. God wants us to redeem shame, turning it into healing.

Living in Freedom

As I write this book I remain aware of all that God has done to take me from shame into freedom. I love living in freedom! The more freedom I have, the more freedom I can pass on to others. In sharing this information on shame, I realize what a powerful negative impact shame has had in my life.

God gave my parents six children in six years, including two sets of twins. They both married at thirty-four years of age. My father served in the Canadian army in the Second World War and he was wounded in 1943 in Sicily. After a two-year convalescence in England he returned to Canada to marry my mother, whom he had known for eighteen years. During those eighteen years, my mother practiced nursing. After they married, they began raising a family.

My parents' firstborn is my sister named Judy. Next came my

brother, Grant, and me (although I came first, being eight minutes older). Two-and-a-half years later, Ross was born; two-and-a-half years after that, Lynne and Elaine, my twin sisters, were born. As Christians, my parents sought God for His help in raising our family. It was a good family, but not a perfect one. However, I wrestled with feelings of insecurity personally. I also struggled with a sense of inferiority toward my twin brother, Grant. Looking back, I realize my feelings of inferiority were not the fault of my brother, who was my best friend growing up. Although my inferiority feelings were a lie, I believed that deception for many years.

During my growing years I felt I had to compete with my brother, yet I could never win in such a competition. Now I know that I was never expected to compete with him. I was created unique, as is everyone. Comparing myself to anyone else is a lie from the pit. Also, I inherited insecurity from my parents, which aided the lie of inferiority being formed in me.

As a child, I remember being afraid to do many things. Despite wanting to try different things I was intimidated by people, and therefore functioned in bouts of shyness. Often self-conscious and ashamed of myself, I didn't really like many things about myself. At that time, I had no idea that these were shame issues. Later during my college and university years, I struggled with low self-esteem. Not until I began studying this subject of shame did I realize that all of my struggles with insecurity, inadequacy, low self-esteem, and inferiority were shame issues.

I lacked self-confidence because I didn't like myself. As a result of my personal battle with shame, I feel a call on my life to bring freedom to people from this area of shame. Shame robs us of the power of God in our lives and steals our God-given destiny. Where shame is functioning, we are deprived of God's creative capacity.

Symbolically, shame casts our eyes downward to the ground. Literally, people struggling with shame often walk with their heads down. They are focused on surviving in the present and do not see the future that God has planned for them. Insecurity causes them to be self-conscious and self-centred. They fail to see the possibilities available.

Shame and Disgrace

Nineteen times in Scripture the words *shame* and *disgrace* are used together. The word *disgrace* means the removal of grace. I define the word *grace* as God's empowering presence. It is the presence of God in our lives, accompanied by His power in the form of grace, which enables us to achieve what God has called us to do. We tend to confuse grace with mercy.

Mercy is defined as not receiving the punishment I deserve. But mercy also means receiving what I should not have been given; that is, forgiveness. Because of our sin and rebellion we should have been punished; that is, we should not have received forgiveness. Mercy extends forgiveness where it is not merited. Combined with the power of grace mercy lifts me up, thereby enabling me to receive the Holy Spirit to empower me to do what God wants.

The prefix *dis* means the negation of, the reversal of, or removal of something. Disgrace is the removal of grace or power in our lives, wherever shame is functioning. Wherever shame controls us, God's grace has been removed from that area of our lives.

An example appears in Isaiah 30:1–5 (NIV). In this chapter, Isaiah is prophesying to the people of Judah. Assyria was their mortal enemy during this period. The mighty nation of Assyria defeated nation after nation in war; Judah was next in their sights. Assyria was the prevailing political power; Judah, by comparison, was tiny. In order to protect themselves from the Assyrians, the political leaders of Judah turned to Egypt as an ally. Instead of turning to God for protection, they relied on the power of Egypt. The prophet Isaiah challenges the people of Judah, saying:

> "Woe to the obstinate children," declares the Lord, "to those who carry out plans that are not mine, forming an alliance, but not by my Spirit, heaping sin upon sin; who go down to Egypt without consulting me; who look for help to Pharaoh's protection, to Egypt's shade for refuge."

Egypt, the second ranking power of the time, was a natural choice for Judah to seek help against Assyria. But Isaiah says:

> "But Pharaoh's protection will be to your shame, Egypt's shade will bring you disgrace. Though they have officials in Zoan and their envoys have arrived in Hanes, everyone will be put to shame because of a people useless to them, who bring them neither help nor advantage, but only shame and disgrace."

Judah had already sent envoys to Egypt to negotiate this political alliance. Isaiah says to the nation of Judah everyone involved in this political process will be put to shame. Don't put your trust in the Egyptians; put your trust in God. Instead of asking God for help, Judah, to their shame, sought to solve their fear of Assyria through their own wisdom and resources. Instead of seeking God's help, they obstinately rebelled against God.

So God removed His presence; and because of their shame, God removed His power to help them fight Assyria. Later when Hezekiah becomes king, the nation turns back to God for help because of the king's spiritual leadership.

Whenever we live outside the will and purposes of God, we, too, will eventually experience shame and disgrace. When we hide from God (shame), He will remove His power and presence from us in areas where we try to hide from Him.

CHAPTER 2

THE MANY FACES OF SHAME

Because shame is the most hidden of all the emotions, many people cannot identify with it. In fact, many people have no idea that they have shame issues in their lives even when their lives are dominated by shame. To help us identify with shame, I want to provide some stories that you may find relevant. Hopefully, you will see in your own lives what will help you identify with shame.

Years ago when I was the chairman of counselling services at Lethbridge College, I shared a joke with my colleagues just before the doors were to be opened for the students to come in. We had just hired a new employee in our department. I was telling a joke that had an ethnic slant to it. It concerned Jewish and Scottish people known for their frugality. As I told the joke, I looked at my new employee to see the look of dismay on her face. I realized that she probably was Jewish or Scottish; I felt my face go red, my body get hot, and I started to perspire. I knew I had created an offense with my ethnic joke. Although I quickly apologized, I still felt the shame of the unkindness of my ethnic slur (I really knew better and telling the joke was against my conscience).

Shame can also occur when we act foolishly before a large audience or even small audience. Have you ever been in that situation? You think, *I'll never allow myself to get into that mess again.*

One of my responsibilities as a counsellor and as chairman of counselling services was preparing student graduates to receive their diplomas at graduation ceremonies. We lined up the students according to their faculties, then in alphabetical order. As their names were called, the students, in caps and gowns, marched across the stage to receive their hard-earned recognition. As they received their diplomas and handshakes, the family members and friends would cheer for them. The audience was quite large and ranged from 1,500 to 2,000 people.

Many of the students, standing in line waiting for their names to be called, would mutter under their breath, "I hope I don't trip." Everybody was aware of the shame that would befall if they were to stumble while crossing the stage. Although few students stumbled, occasionally someone tripped and felt ashamed.

The Shame of First Experiences

Shame can also arise from an act that is considered stupid in front of peers or people who make us feel insecure. After graduating from high school, I got my first "real" full-time job. I worked in downtown Vancouver, B.C., at a firm called Pemberton Securities. It was a brokerage firm dealing in stocks, bonds, and financial investments. At age seventeen, I was insecure and unsure of myself in an adult world.

My job as the office boy was to deliver messages and mail from one department to another in this large financial firm. I remember that carrying a million dollars in stocks and bonds from one office building to another made me nervous. But I felt even more insecurity trying to get people's names right. When I called someone by the wrong name or delivered mail to the wrong party, the office folks teased me. I remember struggling, not wanting to go to work, because my inadequacy made me feel ashamed.

Many shame experiences we carry into adult life occur in childhood. These embarrassing events can scar us for years, yet we may not know the full extent of the damage to our psyches until years later. In grade one I had a shame experience that impacted me for years although I did not know its cause.

My grade one teacher was gentle and kind. One day, it seems she was having a bad day. In the back of our 1950's classroom there were cloakrooms for students' jackets and rubber boots on rainy days. These cloakrooms had blackboards that would slide up and down and could serve as additional chalkboards (I know, I know, this was a long time ago).

On this particular day, when a student went to get something from the cloakroom, the noise of the blackboard moving caught the class's attention; everyone turned around to see the disturbance. The teacher told the class to pay attention, keeping their eyes to the front. For some reason or other I kept my eyes focused on the back, mesmerized by the distraction. I have no idea why I did this. Finally, the teacher said to me, "Hey, rubberneck, turn around." I think she must have been having a frustrating day.

Of course, I was embarrassed and I turned fifty shades of red. I forgot about this incident shortly afterward, but the wound was much greater than I realized. How do I know this? I thought for years there must be something wrong with my neck. I believed it must be elongated and misshapen. I realized this years later when my older children were in their teen years. They would say, "Dad, why do you never wear t-shirts?" I would dismiss their question and say, "I don't know, I just prefer collars on my shirts."

One day, I asked the Holy Spirit the reason I never wore t-shirts. Out of the blue this memory of my grade one class came flooding into my mind. I would never have connected these two issues, but suddenly it made sense. I felt I had to cover my neck because something was wrong with it; I thought it was too long.

With this realization I acknowledged my anger toward my teacher, forgiving her for her thoughtless comment. That simple comment scarred me for years; in my shame I never wore t-shirts. Although not aware of the impact this comment had, it affected my behaviour in this specific way. Today I love to wear t-shirts when I am dressing casually. Most likely this story has raised some awareness of your own memories. If you are connecting some of the dots in your past family experiences, that is good.

The Shame of Experiencing Someone Else's Shame

Sometimes, shame experiences of the past result from reacting to someone else's shame and then reacting to your own shame. When I was growing up, every summer my parents took us to my aunt's cottage at Boundary Bay, near the Canadian-American border in the lower mainland of British Columbia. In those days, in order to get to Boundary Bay we would have to take a short ferry ride across the Fraser River, whereas today the Deas Tunnel has now replaced that ferry ride.

One particularly hot summer day, returning from our three-week vacation, we were waiting in a long line of cars for the ferry ride. As the cars from the ferry disembarked we sat in this lineup of cars, watching them go on the other side of the road. I have no idea what got into me—perhaps I was bored—but I yelled out the word *sucker* at the cars which were passing in the opposite lane. My father, thoroughly embarrassed at my behaviour, reached from the front seat to swat me in the backseat. His shame at his son's senseless behaviour caused him to strike at me.

Naturally, my reaction to my father's angry outburst was shame at my stupidity. Sometimes, one shame incident will have enough impact to affect us for years to come. Other times, the accumulated effect of many smaller incidents of shameful behaviour carries the impact in our lives. For example, being called *stupid* repeatedly develops an accumulated effect on our self-esteem.

Being Shamed by Others

Perhaps you also can relate to this experience. When you enter a bookstore to purchase a book, you discover a table with a sign on it which says, "All books on this table —25% off marked prices." You pick up four books; three of them have red labels but one of the books doesn't. The store clerk takes 25 percent off the three books but fails to discount the book with no red label.

As you are walking out of the store, you suddenly realize the clerk failed to give you 25 percent off for the unmarked book. You go back to the clerk, telling him he failed to give you your 25 percent discount. He looks at you disdainfully and in a loud voice says, "So you want your dollar back, do you!" Everyone in the store stares at you; you can feel your temperature rising and your face turning red. You walk out of the store "feeling like two cents," vowing never to return to this store again. You have just been shamed or punished for wanting your discount.

Here's another scenario you may have experienced. You are invited to a party. You are quite delighted by the invitation because these are people you respect. The night of the party, you decide to wear your best casual clothes. With your partner you arrive, knock on the door, and are invited in by the hostess. As you enter you suddenly realize that everyone else is dressed formally while you are dressed casually. Nobody told you it was a formal affair.

As you enter the room, all eyes turn to you to see who has just arrived. You wish you could sink through a hole in the floor because of your embarrassment. You feel totally out of place. You want to turn around and leave immediately, but your legs won't cooperate with what your mind is telling you to do. You think to yourself, *I feel so foolish and out of place. I wish someone had told me the dress code for the evening.*

These examples are some of the faces of shame. Are you grasping a little more of what shame is? Can you relate to these experiences to your life?

CHAPTER 3

SHAME – THE MASTER EMOTION

In psychological circles, shame is referred to as the "master emotion." When I first saw that term during my research on shame, I thought the researchers were exaggerating. But the more I explored this subject of shame, Biblically and psychologically, the more I became convinced this term is accurate. The power of shame is the unconscious regulator of many of our behaviours. Shame influences all our other emotions and yet it is the most private of all emotions. We are painfully unaware of the impact of shame on our daily living.

Here's a thought-provoking question: in conversations with family, friends, colleagues, and neighbours, how often does the subject of shame come up? Rarely! More commonly the subject of fear is discussed, or even guilt—which is also uncommon because we have been taught by our society that guilt should not be discussed. Virtually nobody talks about shame except in a counselling session—even then it doesn't come up for discussion very often.

Shame experiences in childhood can so mar the personality that its impact is felt for a lifetime. Interestingly, these shame scars can be so hidden that we do not know what is affecting our behaviour. We may wonder all our lives what causes our behaviour, never realizing it is due to unhealed shame. Sometimes people cannot motivate themselves to carry out certain behaviours. They are not aware it is the result of the accusations of shame in their unconscious memories.

I have never forgotten counselling a young woman in her late twenties who had been sexually abused in childhood by four of her family members—a father, an uncle, and two brothers. She was an exceptionally attractive woman. Her good looks and beautiful figure likely contributed to her family taking advantage of her. It wasn't her fault for the way God had made her, but she hated herself because of it.

As a result of this abuse, she could not accept any compliments about her beauty or even about whom she is as a person. She saw herself as trash through the eyes of shame. In fact, it was her husband who pleaded with her to go to counselling. He was confused, even frustrated, at not being able to compliment her. Even when he put a mirror in front of her, she could not see that she is a beautiful woman. So marred by the shame of her abuse, she couldn't see the truth of who she is as a woman.

A Negative View of Life

Shame can produce such a negative view that all of our positive attributes are eclipsed by the negative view we have of ourselves. To feel shame is more than to feel guilty about certain behaviours. When we feel ashamed, we use expressions such as: I feel ugly, stupid, phony, ignorant, cheap, insignificant, immature, unlovely, unworthy. We see ourselves as grasping, boring, dreary, dull, monotonous, unexciting, and tedious. These are common shame words in the unconscious vocabulary of people who are hurting.

We may never allow others, or even ourselves, to acknowledge this shame, but we live with the consequences of hiding from this negative shame. Sometimes, when shame issues are brought to our attention, we vigorously deny them. We resist even hearing these words. As we will see later, shame can cause a great deal of anger during our attempts to protect ourselves from these shame experiences coming to light.

However, in my Biblical and psychological research I discovered, to my surprise, that not all shame is negative. Shame can have a positive side. Positive shame is like breathing. In fact, you can't exist without it. It's necessary for a healthy emotional life. One of the things I love to do when I am counselling people caught in their shame lifestyles is to work at turning negative shame to positive shame. We will cover positive shame in more detail later in the book.

Negative shame is pathogenic; that is, it kills. A pathologist is someone who examines cadavers or dead bodies to see what the cause of death was. He studies diseases and then does autopsies on deceased people to see what caused their death. People with pathogenic shame in their emotional systems have the potential to die through suicide.

In psychological studies, shame is an important element in issues like rage, sexual abuse, addictions, depression, obsessive compulsive disorders, sexual dysfunction, and eating disorders, to name a few. Although many more factors than shame cause these disorders, shame plays a major role in the ongoing battle with these maladies.

Much of Shame Is Repressed

Much of our shame is repressed—that is, buried within our psyche because we are "ashamed" of our shame. This is why it is often so difficult to deal with shame issues. We don't want to examine the shame of which we are so ashamed. We don't like shame and we don't want to think about it. We don't even want to be taught about it. A great deal of our emotional energy is actually designed to help us dodge the shameful experiences we have repressed. We don't even know we are repressing these thoughts or emotions because repression is unconscious to us.

I remember vividly I was counselling another woman who had significant shame issues. She had been physically abused, primarily by her mother. She grew up on a farm. Her mother was supremely unloved by her husband. I suspect that the mother came from an abusive home herself. My counsellee told me that one day her mother dragged her from the barn to the house by her ponytail. She was physically abused many times because of her mother's anger and shame.

Her mother constantly called her a slut even though this young woman was an attractive, innocent person. In a perverted way, her mother was trying to restrain her daughter from a lifestyle of sexually inappropriate behaviour. However, the opposite occurred. The more the mother called her daughter a slut, the more the daughter identified herself as one.

This woman had come to the counselling centre where I was working to deal with a number of issues in her life. She was a born-again Christian but she had been living with a man, knowing it was wrong. She desperately wanted to be married to him; but after years when marriage didn't happen, she chose to live with him.

When she came to see me she had left this man but was still burdened by significant shame. Her struggle revolved around this identity of being called a "slut." As I got to know her, it seemed obvious to me that she dressed seductively in hopes of attracting a man. Her skirts were short and tight, and her blouses were also form fitting. She attempted to attract men but in all the wrong ways.

I talked with my wife Sherry about it one day and said I really needed to address this issue. Today I wouldn't counsel a woman alone, but in those days I was counselling professionally at a counselling centre. My wife thought it was all right for me to address this woman with my concerns about her clothes. So one day I cautiously talked to her about the way she dressed. Was she aware that she was attracting the wrong kind of attention? She was living out of the shame identity that her mother had wrongfully given her, even though she didn't want to live that way.

Through tears she acknowledged her shame and her anger toward her mother. She realized she was making wrong choices in life. She then was able to repent of the lie that her worth came from expressing her sexuality in a seductive manner. This shame from childhood was affecting the adult choices she made for many years. It influenced the way she viewed herself and how she related to men.

Ashamed of Our Shame

Misunderstood sexuality is only one way shame can be expressed. I have seen shame expressed in many different ways. For example, a person who is significantly overweight boards a bus. As the bus travels its route, it gets more crowded. However, this large person is now taking up two seats because of size. He may try to disguise his shame, but he is clearly aware of the implications of his size on a crowded bus. Shame is like a distant beating drum playing in the background, always haunting him with this shame. Whether male or female this shame plays on the mind, and the shame identity has great impact on self-esteem.

Sigmund Freud used the picture of an iceberg to illustrate how the conscious, subconscious—which he called the preconscious—and the unconscious aspects of our psyche interact. I have included a similar iceberg diagram in Appendix 1 to illustrate the effect that shame from our subconscious and unconscious has on our conscious awareness. While ninety percent of an iceberg lies below the surface of the ocean, only ten percent extends above the waterline. An iceberg is a good illustration of how much the subconscious and unconscious, which we are mostly unaware of, impacts our conscious behaviour.

In the conscious realm, shame produces self-hatred. But in the subconscious just below the surface it can produce self-doubt, which ultimately affects our behaviour and especially how we interact in social settings. But when shame is repressed further into the unconscious, it causes a variety of emotional disturbances. Unconscious shame can express itself in forms of defiance, rebellion, addictions, withdrawal, or perfectionism, to name a few.

This gnawing shame can be working in our psyche without us being aware of its insidious impact. Unless someone opens a discussion about it, we only have a vague sense (that distant beating drum) of something going on inside. That's because in our North American culture, shame is seldom discussed. In other cultures, like Asia or Africa, shame behaviours may be more prevalent; nevertheless, shame is not discussed any more than in Western society.

A hundred years ago parents warned their children not to bring shame to the family name; behaviours like adultery, hidden illegitimate children, cowardice, incest, bad manners or laziness. I remember being warned by my mother to make sure I wore clean underwear when I travelled, in case of an accident and the ambulance driver or doctor or nurse would discover this.

We are greatly ashamed to talk about our shame issues. Shame is not an acceptable topic of conversation in a public setting. Shame is a serious issue for alcoholics. In fact, shame was part of the motivation for Bill Wilson and Dr. Bob Smith of Akron, Ohio, to launch Alcoholics Anonymous. They wanted to provide a safe place where it was acceptable to talk about the shame of being an alcoholic. They devised a program, the 12-Step Program, to talk about the shame of excessive drinking without feeling ashamed. They made it a safe environment to discuss someone's background and why he fell into alcoholism. People who had been alcoholics found recovery by openly talking about the reason they drank.

Why is shame so difficult a topic for people to converse? Because shame has enormous power over us, more than most of us understand.

CHAPTER 4

AHITHOPHEL'S STORY

A classic illustration of shame's power is found in the Bible. This story found in 2 Samuel 15–17 concerns a man named Ahithophel. Ahithophel was one of David's wise counsellors, maybe his wisest counsellor. David's son, Absalom, fourth in line to the throne and popular in Israel, had murdered his brother, Amnon, because Amnon had raped Absalom's sister, Tamar. Because David didn't punish Amnon for this rape, Absalom took matters into his own hands. Absalom is furious at his brother, Amnon, for the shame he brought on his sister, Tamar. So a while later, Absalom puts on a party for all his siblings and many other friends. He includes Amnon, perhaps to appear as a goodwill gesture. When Amnon was drunk, Absalom orders his men to kill Amnon, which they did.

Absalom then flees the country to avoid the wrath of his father David. For three years he stays with Talmai, the king of Geshur. Although David wanted to get in touch with Absalom, he didn't until Joab, his top general, forced his hand through trickery. With David's permission, Joab brought Absalom back to Jerusalem but David refused to see him. This estrangement continued for two years, until Absalom pressed Joab to arrange a face-to-face meeting with David.

Although the Bible doesn't state this, it appears that Absalom was tired of his father's indecisive manner of ruling the country. He became increasingly angry. So he started a conspiracy against his father, King David, to take over the throne. Absalom sat outside the gates of Jerusalem and dispensed justice to the people, something apparently David was not doing.

Eventually, Absalom gathered 200 leading men from Jerusalem at Hebron and proclaimed himself king. Among those he invited was Ahithophel, David's loyal counsellor and personal friend. The Bible doesn't say why, but Ahithophel decided to change his loyalty from David to Absalom. David receives a report that the hearts of the people are now with Absalom.

When David hears about this full-scale mutiny, he flees for his life. Leaving Jerusalem, he crossed the Kidron Valley and headed for the desert with a company of people loyal to him. David left behind in Jerusalem ten of his concubines to care for the palace. David also asked Zadok and Abiathar, two of his loyal priests, to stay in Jerusalem. They also returned the ark of the covenant, which David had taken on his escape. Along with their two sons, the priests were to act as spies so David coult track Absalom's actions. David was told that his friend, Ahithophel, joined the conspirators, so he prayed, "O Lord, turn Ahithophel's counsel into foolishness" (2 Samuel 15:31 NIV).

To help David, Hushai the Arkite also went back to Jerusalem to frustrate the advice of Ahithophel and send any information via Zadok and Abiathar's two sons, Ahimaaz and Jonathan. The story becomes a real cloak-and-dagger narrative of spies, intrigue, and narrow escapes. When Absalom arrives in Jerusalem, he seeks Ahithophel's advice.

Ahithophel tells Absalom to sleep with his father's concubines so that the people will know that Absalom is serious about his conspiracy, making it obvious that he has "burned his bridges." Absalom follows Athiophel's advice and has sex with the ladies on the palace roof so everyone knows what he has done; he cannot turn back now.

The Bible says of Ahithophel in 2 Samuel 16:23 (NIV): "Now in those days the advice Ahithophel gave was like that of one who inquires of God. That was how both David and Absalom regarded all of Ahithophel's advice." When Ahithophel spoke, everyone listened.

Again Absalom sought out Ahithophel for his advice for the next step in the conspiracy. Ahithophel told Absalom to set out immediately after David with 12,000 of his best soldiers and attack him while David is weak and weary. But God puts it in Absalom's heart to also summon Hushai the Arkite, David's friend. He asked him for his advice as well. Hushai was also known for his great wisdom. Obviously God is still very much in control, despite Absalom thinking of himself as in control.

Hushai countered Ahithophel's sage advice by saying that David is a fierce and experienced warrior, even though he is older and less virile—he is like a mother bear robbed of her cubs. In essence, Hushai cautioned him not to underestimate his father. He told Absalom to gather all the men from Dan in the north to Beersheba in the south. "Form a large army," says Hushai, "and then attack David so Absalom will be sure to win this civil war." These instructions give David time to flee then organize the people loyal to him to fight Absalom.

Absalom and his other counsellors accepts Hushai's advice, because the Lord wanted to frustrate the good advice of Ahithophel in order to bring disaster upon Absalom. Jonathan and Ahimaaz, the two young spies, sneak out of Jerusalem to tell David. En route they hide in an old, dry well to escape detection. They finally reached David to tell him of Absalom's plan.

In 2 Sam. 17:23 (NIV), the Bible says, "When Ahithophel saw that his advice had not been followed, he saddled his donkey and set out for his house in his hometown. He put his house in order and then hanged himself. So he died and was buried in his father's tomb."

My first thought was: *Doesn't suicide seem like an extreme overreaction just because once, someone didn't take your wise advice? What made Ahithophel do this?* The answer is: shame! When I checked the meaning of Ahithophel's name, I discovered something very interesting. His name means "brother of foolish talk." Many of the names given to Hebrew children were given prophetically or because of something that the parents sensed about their character. Here's what I think happened. I can only share my presumption because the Scripture is silent.

I think that all of Ahithophel's life he was trying to prove that he was not just a silly boy from whom came much foolishness. He may have been one of the younger sons in the family. He struggled internally against the lie that he was a foolish boy. In the process of trying to prove his family and others wrong he compensated by developing a great deal of wisdom, for which he became famous. But his wisdom was motivated by shame.

When his advice was not taken by Absalom on this one occasion, Ahithophel was so shamed that he made a choice to end his life. As previously mentioned, deep shame is pathogenic. In Ahithophel's case, shame literally killed him. In many cases it may not kill but cripples our courage, destroys our creativity, and eradicates our destiny. Shame has tremendous power over us, yet most of us have no idea of the power of shame in our lives.

CHAPTER 5

SHAME'S POWER OVER US

Do we ever ask ourselves the question: "I wonder what I might have become if...?" "If I only hadn't...." These questions often indicate areas of shame in us, operating through our unconscious. Shame can cause us to do appalling destruction to our lives.

On April 28, 1999, a young man named Jason Lang was shot by a fellow student who had dropped out of school earlier in the year at the W.R. Myers High School in Taber, Alberta, Canada. We were acquaintances of his parents, Dale and Diane Lang, at the time. Dale was the pastor of St. Theodores, a small charismatic Anglican church in Taber, a small town of 5,000 people, 30 minutes drive from Lethbridge where we live.

The day after the tragedy took place, I appeared on a Christian television station discussing the event and praying for the Lang family. As a result of seeing me on television, I was invited by some of the youth leaders at St. Theodores to help them process all the grief, anger, and confusion that this murder had created. It was a large media event across Canada at the time.

Sherry and I drove to Taber to meet with this church youth group expecting fifteen, but instead about fifty young people attended, plus some parents. We discussed how to deal with their anger and process their grief. The young man who had shot Jason with a rifle had an older brother who was also at the meeting. He talked with us at some length. He was experiencing great anger and shame at what his brother had done to the family name and reputation.

Here is what I sensed motivated this fourteen-year-old young man to commit this crime. He was full of shame from incessant bullying, which led to a great deal of internalized anger. He was teased unmercifully, laughed at, and made fun of by his fellow students. The bullying was so intense for him that he dropped out of school to be homeschooled. The shame of this treatment accumulated in him until the day it exploded in an act of rage. He didn't deliberately go after Jason or the other student. But he walked into his high school and, with a rifle, randomly shot two students, killing Jason and injuring this other student.

Because it became a national news event covered by all Canadian telivision stations, Dale Lang had an amazing opportunity to express publicly his and Diane's forgiveness toward this boy. As a result of this personal tragedy, Dale received numerous invitations to share this message of forgiveness in schools across Canada.

The Power of Unresolved Shame

I believe unresolved shame is the driving force—although not the only issue—behind most addictions. One of the issues that holds men—and some women—trapped in pornography is shame. They feel so ashamed that they lose control over this perverse sexuality. For women, and some men, overeating clearly connects to shame. While people live in these hidden areas of shame, the only factor that mitagates against these shame feelings is the very addictions that they despise.

Whether aware or not, we carry constant anxiety about our shame. The only way we can feel better about ourselves is to do something to overcome the shame, and this leads us into addictive patterns. Then we feel the shame of getting caught in the cycle of the addiction and feel worse about ourselves. To avoid feeling shame, we return to the addiction again and the cycle continues. We end up with anxiety or undefined fear that prevents us from doing what we love to do, and conversely what we don't want to do.

I remember as a child daydreaming about standing before audiences and dispensing wisdom to them. However, I thought it could never happen because I felt so inadequate and insecure. As I was painfully shy that standing before an audience "freaked me out." Because of my shame, I could not see myself doing public speaking. However, through overcoming my shame, I now fulfill my destiny to teach in numerous places throughout the world.

Shame's Control over Our Behaviours

A man came to see me for counselling. His present problem was tension in his marriage. He knew he was dealing with anger problems in his own life. One of the tensions in his marriage involved this man's refusal to take his wife to a restaurant for dinner. I asked him about his family origin. His mother was from a well-to-do family and trained in good manners and decorum. Late in her adolescence, she went through a period of rebellion toward her father. As a result, she married a good-looking, athletic man who was from a much lower economic class against her father's wishes.

In time they had two children, a boy and a girl. The mother was determined that her son (my counsellee) would not grow up to be unmannerly and boorish like his father. When she married him, he was a "hunk." But in time, he became a "boor" in her mind. The mother used shame on her son to try to keep him from being unmannerly at the table like his father.

So as the son entered his twenties and thirties, he was carrying both shame and anger toward his mother about his eating habits. This was the reason he never went out to eat in public. We had to work through the anger toward both his parents and expose the lies that were part of the shaming process he carried in growing up. Shame has incredible power over us. We often don't know where it originates from in our past.

Shame's Contagion

Shame has a contagious quality. We feel shameful in looking at another person's shame. Reviewing another's shame in itself creates shame, which is why it is so difficult to talk about shame or even write about it. I know that when I first started to explore this subject and research it, my own "shame demons" stirred. But if we want freedom from shame we have to reveal the shame topics, opening them up from where they lie hidden. Wherever we are not free, wherever we are locked up inside ourselves, I am certain we have some hidden shame issues lurking in our past.

My principal motivation for writing this book is to bring greater freedom to all people, especially those who are imprisoned by shame. I love to see people filled with the Holy Spirit, but when we are filled with shame, the Holy Spirit can't rule in our lives. We have to bring our shame to the cross. Then we are ready for our own "Pentecost" and the empowering of the Holy Spirit.

I want to conclude this section of the book with a prayer. If you feel inclined to pray this prayer along with me, please do. Pray with full sincerity of your heart. This first step tells God you want to start on this journey of getting free from shame.

Prayer: *Father, I want to be free of anything that holds me back from becoming the man or woman that You have called me to be.*

- I give You the key to my closet of shame, and I ask You to be gentle with me but also thorough in exposing and cleaning out my shame.

- I declare my trust in You as my Saviour and Lord, and I open my heart to begin a journey of your cleansing love. Amen.

PART 2

DEFINING SHAME
BIBLICALLY

CHAPTER 6

WHAT IS SHAME?

Most people know the word *shame* but have trouble defining it. Most have a vague notion of shame, but when asked for a definition, they struggle to put the words together. I want to give a clear and precise definition of *shame* that everyone can grasp and "take home in his back pocket," so to speak. I am taking my definition primarily from the Scriptures, then adding some points from psychology.

The first recorded use of the word *shame* in the Bible is found in Genesis 2:25 (NIV). "The man and his wife were both naked and they felt no shame." There are three key words in this verse. The first is the word *naked*. When God created Adam and Eve, they lived in innocence with nothing to hide. Because they had nothing to hide, they didn't feel ashamed of their bodies and didn't need to cover them. They lived in a perfect environment and, in that milieu, they accepted their bodies completely. Even though they were naked, Adam and Eve were not aware of a shameful experience, because their minds were pure and free of sin. Negative shame means hiding what we deem wrong about ourselves.

Emotionally Healthy Marriages

In an emotionally healthy marriage, husbands and wives each should feel the same way about their own body as their spouse's body. No shame feelings should arise when standing naked before one's spouse. Now I recognize that many come into marriage with distorted ideas about sexuality; we may have prior experiences that warped our perspective about our bodies. Unfortunately, because we have seen too many "perfect" bodies in movies, books, magazines, and the internet, we know our bodies are far from "perfect." Because of comparisons, we often don't like our bodies. But that attitude is a lie from a world that deceived us.

God created marriage for the enjoyment of sexuality; He set the boundaries of marriage as the only place to enjoy naked bodies in innocence. Before sin entered the picture, nakedness was acceptable. Negative shame caused us to hide. In the innocence of the Garden of Eden, nothing needed hiding. Shame was unnecessary at this point in creation.

Shame Is an Emotion

The second key word in verse 25 is the word *felt*. Shame is an emotion. It is part of our affective system and is designed by God to act as a signal. All emotions are signals, awakening us to something that needs our attention. When we feel afraid, we are meant to pay attention to our fear in case there is danger that needs to be addressed. God designed guilt feelings to alert us to areas where we have sidestepped the path of right living, so we can repent. God wants to prevent us from suffering the consequences of sin.

Shame's positive signal alerts us to what is appropriate to hide from others—our naked bodies. When we live in positive shame, we dress fittingly. I wear clothing in public so I do not embarrass myself, or others. Negative shame also sends us signals. It reminds us of areas in our lives that are not properly worked out, so we try to hide those areas. When we feel shame, we need to ask ourselves what we feel we need to hide. Negative shame works as a signal to help us see areas of our lives that need to be worked through because we are not free in those areas.

Here is an example of what I am talking about. Men frequently come to me to overcome their struggle with pornography. But they do not come for counselling until shame makes them desperate enough to acknowledge their need for help. Every man I have seen in this area of struggle feels huge shame for this failure. Although the shame is overwhelming, and initially stops them from coming for counselling, eventually shame is the very thing that causes them to reach out for help.

In the innocence of Eden, Adam and Eve had no need for the emotional signal of shame. There was no sin in the Garden, or in their lives. Nothing required hiding. They had not yet crossed the one boundary God set for them, which was to stay away from the Tree of the Knowledge of Good and Evil. Because they had not yet rebelled against God's command, they had never experienced shame.

To Be Shamed Is to Be Uncovered

The third key word in verse 25 is the word *shame*. The primary meaning of the Hebrew word *shame* is to fall into disgrace, normally through failure or defeat at the hands of an enemy. It expresses a sense of confusion and dismay when things turn out contrary to one's expectations. **To experience shame is to be uncovered.**

Prior to sin entering the world, Adam and Eve felt no need to cover up. They had no knowledge of either shame or guilt. But when Adam and Eve disobeyed God's command by rebelling against God, they experienced both shame and guilt. Believe it or not, God introduced those signals to protect them from ongoing rebellion and sin. Although God gave Adam and Eve these shame and guilt signals to protect them, Satan used those emotional signals against them.

Appendix 2 summarizes, in diagram form, the concept of shame in the Scriptures. You will notice that shame is primarily defined in negative terms because of how we generally experience shame. Shame is dominated by its negative side. But God wants to turn negative shame into positive shame to help us deal with sin. *Shame* is defined as *a powerful emotion caused by an awareness or deficiency in character or behaviour that leaves a person feeling uncovered*. A more succinct definition of negative shame is: *a feeling of needing to hide something*. However, shame can function both positively and negatively. Positive shame is defined as a wholesome attitude that helps define and shape a character of nobility, honour, and integrity.

Positive Shame versus Negative Shame

One Biblical example for how shame is used positively is found in Luke 16:3 (NIV). "The manager said to himself, 'What shall I do now? My master is taking away my job. I'm not strong enough to dig, and I'm too ashamed to beg....'" This man has been dishonest with his master's finances and has been discovered. He is being fired and is caught in a dilemma. He's accustomed to living a good life, serving nobility, but now he can't lower himself to live a life of begging. Because of his shame, he uses his ingenuity to make friends with his master's debtors by cutting all of them a deal (on his master's money). Now they will be beholden to him and willing to help him when his master lets him go.

Jesus is not validating his dishonesty. He is merely pointing out that the people of the world are shrewder in dealing with their own kind than are "people of the light." This man used his shame to find a way to take care of himself. Positive shame is like breathing air—necessary for life. God designed positive shame to bring repentance from sin. God uses shame to bring people to Himself.

Negative shame is defined as *a conscious or unconscious feeling of self-hatred, in one or more areas of life that is like an unhealed wound in the soul.* Unacknowledged shame is destructive. It is like a locked door to the soul. It blocks the creative potential of your destiny and it is used in a destructive way against you. Sometimes, because we don't have enough shame, we don't repent. Ignoring positive shame causes more negative shame. I have seen this phenomenon in people wrestling with addictions. They have to be desperate enough to break the cycle of their addictive behaviour.

Jeremiah 6:15 (NIV) tells us that we need shame to help us stop sinning against God in ways that are self-destructive. "Are they ashamed of their detestable conduct? No, they have no shame at all; they do not even know how to blush. So they will fall among the fallen; they will be brought down when I punish them, says the Lord."

To be without shame—to be shameless—is to avoid the restraint of shame, which acts as a guard against sin. We need positive shame to keep us from falling repeatedly into sin. So, positive shame actually aids us in development of godly character. **Positive shame means boundaries.** God gives us boundaries to prevent us from repeating the same mistakes. God did that for Adam and Eve when he put them out of the Garden of Eden, setting an angel with a flaming sword at the boundary of the Garden. Why did He do that? Because He did not want Adam and Eve to eat of the fruit of the Tree of Life and thereby be damned to eternal death, because of their sin of disobeying God when eating from the Tree of the Knowledge of Good and Evil.

The Power of Negative Shame

Negative shame, on the other hand, is a destructive process used by Satan to drive us further from God. **Negative shame causes hiding** when we have acted wrongly. With negative shame, we fear being discovered and rejected by God and others. When we have sinned against God or wronged other people, we feel both guilt and shame. We may try to dismiss or ignore these feelings, but they are functioning in us nevertheless. When we wrong other people, we avoid these people and hide from them. We also try to hide from God, although hiding from Him is impossible.

Amazingly because shame is such a powerful emotion, God Himself uses negative shame against His enemies. The Bible says in

Jeremiah 13:25–27 (NIV), "'This is your lot, the portion I have decreed for you,' declares the Lord, 'because you have forgotten me and trusted in false gods. I will pull up your skirts over your face that your shame may be seen—your adulteries and lustful neighings, your shameless prostitution! I have seen your detestable acts on the hills and in the fields. Woe to you, Jerusalem! How long will you be unclean?'"

Negative shame powerfully attacks the core value of our personhood. When used on us in a negative way, it communicates that we are deficient. **Whereas guilt leads us to examine our negative behaviours, shame leads us to the conclusion that we are a negative person.** Guilt directs us to the behaviours in our lives that need to be changed. Shame is more encompassing than guilt. Unresolved negative shame creates doubt about who we are. We find ourselves hiding our true identity. That which we were uniquely created for is lost, because we are always hiding who we really are.

Instead of using shame as a boundary to prevent us from sin, Satan uses it to push us away from God—and others. Shame keeps us from intimacy with God. When we put our hope in God, we come out from under the "cloak" of negative shame. Deep within us we have real doubts about our ability to ever fully accomplish that unique "something of significance" that we are created for. Because we view ourselves more negatively than positively, we severely limit who we are and who we can become. I will discuss this topic later in the book.

CHAPTER 7

TYPES OF NEGATIVE SHAME

So far we have defined *shame* and have distinguished between negative and positive shame. Along with the difference between the two types of shame are also a number of different kinds of negative shame. This list is not exhaustive, but it will explain different kinds of shame. Let's examine four of them.

Personal Shame

We become aware of personal shame when we have negative experiences in life. We see ourselves in a negative light because of what we believe about ourselves. These experiences will come from our own sin or from being sinned against by others. It leaves us with a sense that we are flawed. We realize that we have stepped across a personal standard that we have set for ourselves (or has been set for us by our family or others). When we violate that standard we experience personal shame. Often we are afraid to examine these violations, because we are ashamed of our shame. So we put the shame experience in the shame closet, because we don't know how to deal with it.

I counselled with a man who came to me after his wife had previously come for counselling to work out her side of the marriage conflicts. I asked the wife if her husband would be willing to join us, but she didn't think he would. So, after receiving her permission to call him, I invited him to come for one session to give me his perspective on their marriage. It is rare that a husband refuses to give his side of the story. As a result of that first visit with the husband, we built some trust and he realized he too needed to work through some issues in his own life.

After several sessions with him, we concluded the counselling. With about ten minutes to go, he dropped a bombshell. He told me when he was twenty-three years old he had sexually abused (fondled) three children. Needless to say, I was rather caught off guard and asked him if he wanted to deal with this area of shame in his life. He told me that I was the first person he had ever told. Even his wife did not know at that time. He was about fifty years old and held a position of responsibility in his community.

During our counselling sessions, this man was evaluating me to determine if I could be trusted with the shame that had plagued him for years. He told me that one of his three victims was a neighbour's child—she was fifteen at the time he touched her genitals. The other two were the children of a single-parent mother in another city.

He had long since lost contact with this mother and her two children; therefore, no follow up was possible. But he told me, through his repentance, he was willing to pay for any counselling the neighbour's daughter might need as a result of what he did. I asked him to talk with his wife first and then approach this woman and her husband about what had happened. Of course this abuse had occurred about thirty years earlier, therefore causing difficulty to follow up with what he had done so long ago.

Because he had carried this shame for many years and never dealt with it, his family was impacted in significant ways, even though nobody knew what he had done. This man carried a large fear that he would molest his own children. As a result of this fear, he was emotionally and physically distant from his own children. His daughter was currently pregnant and unmarried; his son was living a rebellious lifestyle with no place for God or the church in his life. The marriage conflicts with his wife were also partly a result of his emotional distance from her.

He saw for the first time how this unresolved shame issue had impacted his family. He had not only violated what he knew the Bible set as a standard but he had also violated his personal standard of right and wrong. Because he was raised in a Christian family, he knew his behaviour was wrong. All his life he was held captive by his shame; his family had paid a high price. As a result of dealing with this shame, he began reestablishing his marriage relationship and reconnecting with both his son and his daughter. I believe the Holy Spirit brought him under conviction and told him he had to deal with this shame from the past. Today he is a free man.

Cultural Shame

Cultural shame is shame imposed on us by expectations of society or culture. These shame feelings arise from such things as a different skin colour from the majority population. It could come from speaking with an accent or being part of a minority religious group. It also could come about from being part of a lower economic or social class. Or we feel ashamed because of our association with the social group we grew up with.

In my first year as a counsellor at Lethbridge College, one of the assignments I was given was to be a counsellor to the First Nations students. Up to this point in my life, I had never had any involvement with aboriginal people in any form. Although I was challenged by this assignment, I also was glad to be stretched and learn about another culture. One day, a First Nations woman who was overseeing the financial aid that the students received asked me to go with her to the reserve where she lived.

I looked forward to visiting the reserve but I experienced something I hadn't expected. For the first time in my life, I was now a minority. My white skin really seemed to stand out; I experienced cultural shame as we toured the reserve. I felt the eyes of people looking at me because I was a visible minority within the majority population. I felt out of place and awkward at that time. It gave me a sensitivity to what many of the First Nations students felt in coming to Lethbridge College, which was dominated by white culture.

Of interest to me today is the many cultures I have met in the previous nineteen years of my life. I have visited more than eighteen countries and loved getting to know many other cultures. I would say, however, that when I was in Kenya speaking in a church of 10,000 people all of whom were dark skinned, I always left feeling like I needed some more sun so I could get a tan! I often told my friends in India how much effort I spent in the summer months trying to look like them.

I remember feeling shame as an evangelical Christian in the public high school I attended in Vancouver, British Columbia. I felt shame because I was different from many of my fellow students. I lived with a different moral standard from others and believed that had I shared my Christian faith, I would have been mocked, although that may not have been true. At church I was told I shouldn't be ashamed of my Christianity; I should be sharing it with my friends. Adding to my shame, I often felt guilty because I knew I shouldn't be ashamed of my beliefs.

Cultural shame is a nagging sense that we are inferior to another group of people. Of course, most of this shame results from believing lies about ourselves, but nevertheless, the shame is real to us. We feel we are not acceptable as we are because we are comparing ourselves to someone else's cultural standard.

.

CHAPTER 8

SOCIAL SHAME

Social shame results from feeling humiliated by violating an accepted social norm. The fear of social shame causes us to ask, when we are invited to a social function, "What's the dress code for this party?" We don't want to shame ourselves by being dressed inappropriately or out of touch with what the majority of people are wearing. Today I am aware that some young people feel the opposite. They feel ashamed if they don't stand out in a social gathering. They purposely want to dress differently to look different. They feel ashamed if they are seen the same as everyone else.

Cultural shame is the shame we feel when someone whispers to us, "Your zipper is down or your dress is caught in the back of your panty hose." We don't like embarrassing ourselves by making a social faux pas or by looking foolish in a social gathering.

After I had worked as a counsellor and the chairman of the counselling department for nine years at Lethbridge College, I transferred to teaching psychology, counselling, and communications. One of the groups of students I taught were nursing students. After teaching one particular class early in the semester—and feeling good about how my lecture went—I experienced some social shame. The students had all left the classroom; I was packing my books, getting ready to leave. I felt a breeze in my midsection and looked down to discover that my zipper had been down for the whole class.

Although none of the students were in the classroom at the time, I felt my face get hot and I knew my face was red. I suppose you could say I experienced "postmortem" shame. I imagined the students whispering to each other, wondering what kind of a "dork" their professor was. Likely nobody even noticed but I felt embarrassed at my social mistake. However, on the positive side, this type of social shame is what prompts most of us to bathe regularly, dress appropriately, eat with manners, and hold our sexual and aggressive impulses in check.

Universal Shame

Generally speaking, psychologists define this type of shame differently. They say universal shame is to be burdened with a festering negative self-portrait, against which one is repeatedly trying to defend. However, I want to define universal shame from a Biblical perspective. I believe it is the condition associated with the fall of man into sin. This type of shame arises from the awareness that we have all failed to do what is right and we are in need of "someone" to save us from our fallen condition. It is this universal shame that fosters the religions of the world. All people are looking for "someone" to save them from this fallen condition. Unless they find the right someone—that is, Jesus— they are going to die in their shame.

In 1998, I was in India teaching at a family church camp. After one of my teaching sessions, I spoke to an elderly Hindu gentleman who was attending the camp because his son, a Christian doctor, had invited him to come. Commonly in India, non-Christians are invited to Christian events because India is a "spiritual" country. This man's son and his son's wife were both Christians, but the father had not yet given his life to Christ. He had just retired from his lifelong job.

As we were talking about retirement, I used this topic as a means to engage him in conversation and to segue into talking about "retirement" in eternity. I said to him, "If you were to die tomorrow, do you think you would go to heaven?" He looked at me and shame came over his face. He said, "I don't think I've lived a good enough life." He was speaking out of his Hindu perspective that works are of crucial importance. I shared the gospel with him. However, I never heard the final results—whether or not he became a Christian. Naturally, I told him he didn't have to work for his salvation. Salvation is a free gift, because Jesus already "worked for it."

Universal shame is the most repressed or hidden of the types of shame. Once a person becomes aware of this deficiency, he begins looking for a "saviour." He may look in all the wrong places, thereby find religion but may also recognize that there is only one "true Saviour" and that is Jesus. He begins to see a need for something more than he presently has. So the enemy tries to repress this type of shame, lest people discover their need of Jesus.

Euphemisms for Shame

Euphemisms are words or expressions we use in place of words that we feel awkward using. Because people are ashamed of their shame, they use substitute words to avoid talking about shame. We don't like examining shame issues; moreover, we don't like using the word *shame*. So we use other words that are more comfortable. Here are some euphemisms for the concept of shame.

> *"It was an awkward moment."*
> *"I am feeling rather guilty."* (We confuse guilt with shame a lot.)
> *"It was an embarrassing situation."* (to feel self-conscious)
> *"It was an uncomfortable feeling."*
> *"He made me feel quite inferior."*
> *"I don't know why I got so anxious."* (We confuse anxiety and shame)
> *"I turned beet red and felt so stupid."*
> *"I felt so sheepish I wanted to drop through the floor."*
> *"I feel so insecure around him or her."*

What Do We Do with Our shame?

As with anger, shame has various degrees. With some shame experiences, our whole body reacts to shame. With other shame experiences, we go into hiding for years. In many shame situations we repress the feelings of shame, but they still accumulate in our "shame closets," only to surface years later.

Shame was introduced into the world because of sin. God wants us to experience freedom from the power of negative shame. Shame can drive us into more sin or more shame, but it can also be used as a signal to keep us from sin. One of my goals in writing this book is to see negative shame turned into positive shame. This transformation is only possible when we acknowledge the areas of hidden shame in our lives. Shame can lead us to repentance and inner change, or shame can lead us to more hiding.

If we find ourselves moving towards hiding shame, we often make silent, unconscious vows never to acknowledge this area of shame again. When we make a mistake that we don't know how to correct, we "close the door" on that mistake, shove it into the "closet of shame," and never learn from it. Shame in our lives is so powerful that we often make vows not to allow anyone to know about our shame. We all have issues from our past of which we feel ashamed (mistakes, sins, and failures). When that happens we lock up those memories, never to examine them again. Unfortunately, these shame secrets still impact us tremendously in our present day lives.

Negative shame has significant bearing in our lives even though much of it is unconscious. We often are not aware of the impact of it in our daily living. We also falsely believe that, because we have hidden our shame from others and from ourselves, we have hidden it from the Almighty. But nothing is hidden from His sight. So to get at these areas of shame, we must intentionally and carefully examine these hidden areas. That's how we turn negative shame into positive shame.

I want to offer you an opportunity now to pray with me if you sense you want to open this area up for some healing and freedom. As I previously said, I offer this prayer carefully and sensitively, aware of its difficulty.

Father, I acknowledge to You that I've closed off certain areas of my life and have never allowed You into them because of my shame about my sin or myself. I'm asking for courage to open the door of shame to You and begin the process of confession, forgiveness, and healing that will set me free in every area of my life.

Amen.

PART 3

THE SOURCE OF SHAME

CHAPTER 9

DEFINITION OF POSITIVE SHAME

As stated earlier, shame exists as a result of sin. This is why shame is primarily defined by its negative traits. Negative shame is characterized by a need to hide something. But God delights in taking what is negative and turning it into something positive for us. Guilt is similar. Like shame, guilt came into our world because of Adam and Eve's sin. But Father God, through His redemptive process, turns guilt into a warning signal to prevent us from falling back into areas of sin repeatedly.

In the Garden of Eden, fear was positive in nature. Fear was called the "fear of the Lord" or reverence for God. It was designed to keep us in awe of a holy God so we would not sin against Him. However, after the Fall, fear also became negative. Adam and Eve tried to hide from God because they became afraid of Him.

Likewise, negative shame causes us to hide from God. But God wants to use this shame to expose what is in us so we can deal with our sin without suffering from its consequences. When we feel uncomfortable about something in our lives, we typically try to hide it from others. God uses positive shame to motivate us to do what is right and to live in right ways. I know I am personally motivated by positive shame because I don't want to stand before the Judgment (Bema) Seat of Christ one day and be ashamed. Instead, I want to be motivated by positive shame. I want to hear God say, "Well done, good and faithful servant."

Because I do not want to be ashamed in His presence, positive shame sets boundaries to keep me from living with unresolved guilt and, therefore, negative shame. If we allow the Holy Spirit, He will take us out of our hiding places and set us in safe places with boundaries that will propel us to live in right ways. That's why positive shame holds great importance to our Christian lives. It is designed to keep us from falling into a life of sin. Positive shame helps keep us on track to live in holiness.

Keeping in mind that shame itself is not positive, it can motivate us in a positive direction to live a life that honours God. A shameless society, which we see increasingly today, creates a world that is becoming substantially more evil. As described in the book of Judges, our world is a world in which "every man did what was right in his own eyes" (Judges 17:6; 21:25 NASB). Without positive shame, chaos fills society.

The Source of Shame

What does the Bible say about why shame exists today? To answer this question, we must return to the Garden of Eden. A reciprocal relationship connects shame with other common emotions like fear, anger, rejection, and guilt. (The word *reciprocal* means to go back and forth; one system feeds the other.) Earlier in this book, I mentioned that psychologists call shame the master emotion, because of the impact shame has on all other emotions.

The malfunctioning of the affective system (like fear, rejection, insecurity, guilt, et cetera) because of the entry of sin into the world is the source of shame. But at the same time, shame creates a malfunctioning of these emotions. Sin's entry into the world turned our emotions upside down. Because of that, we want to hide these emotions that have turned negative. When these emotions' malfunction, they cause shame in us.

Shame's Relationship to Sin

As I previously stated, the first use of the word *shame* in the Bible is in Genesis 2:25 "Adam and his wife were both naked, and they felt no shame." Prior to the entry of sin into the world, in that state of innocence, there was no need for the emotion of shame, either positive or negative.

This story is first told in Genesis 3:6–11 (NIV).

6   When the woman saw that the fruit of the tree was good for food and pleasing to the eye, and also desirable for gaining wisdom, she took some and ate it. She also gave some to her husband, who was with her, and he ate it.

7   Then the eyes of both of them were opened, and they realized they were naked; so they sewed fig leaves together and made coverings for themselves.

8   Then the man and his wife heard the sound of the Lord God as he was walking in the garden in the cool of the day,

and they hid from the Lord God among the trees of the garden.

9   But the Lord God called to the man, 'Where are you?'

10   He answered, 'I heard you in the garden, and I was afraid because I was naked; so I hid.'

11   And he said, 'Who told you that you were naked? Have you eaten from the tree that I commanded you not to eat from?'

Adam did not need a warning of the danger of sin because he lived in perfect innocence. Adam and Eve lived in complete obedience to God's commands, until the serpent deceived them and they believed his lies. When they disobeyed God, guilt was released into their affective systems. They tried to cover up this uncomfortable feeling of guilt by hiding from God. That was the beginning of negative shame.

We live through the same process when we disobey God's commands. When we sense guilt in our emotions but don't deal with our rebellion, we repress the emotional signal and cover guilt up. The moment we sin against God, we sense guilt (unless our consciences have been hardened to block out that signal). If we don't act on the guilt signal we will experience shame, whether or not we are aware of it.

Guilt and Shame

God intends the feeling of guilt to alert us that we have stepped outside of God's righteous boundaries, thereby sinning against Him. Guilt alerts us to repent and reenter God's path of righteousness. When we ignore the guilt signal we hide, just as Adam and Eve did. The guilt then is buried in shame and hidden from our awareness; thus we become covered with shame.

When Adam and Eve stepped aside from the covering that God gave them, choosing to try to be like God in knowing good and evil, they experienced evil for the first time. A sense of shame came upon them. Suddenly, they realized their nakedness and needed to cover up. Adam and Eve sewed clothes from fig leaves for themselves (that makes them history's first tailors). Their actions became the first instance of religious behaviour, because they were trying to employ their own salvation. They tried to correct their own sin problem; we have been trying to cover our own sin ever since. Religion is man's attempt to cover his own guilt and shame.

When God visited them in the cool of the evening, they instinctively hid themselves. Up to this point, they always had looked forward to fellowship with their friend and Creator. If you have raised or are raising children, you have experienced the same thing with your offspring. You walk into a room and immediately sense guilt "written all over their faces." They try to hide their wrong (like they have stolen the proverbial cookie from the cookie jar). Along with the shame and guilt, Adam experienced negative fear in his relationship with God. He became aware that he had rebelled against God's command for him not to eat the fruit from the Tree of the Knowledge of Good and Evil.

In their state of innocence, they enjoyed the freedom of life without clothing. Now they are keenly aware they need to cover up when God comes calling. Any time we find ourselves hiding something from God or trying to hide ourselves from God, we must ask: what is God alerting me to that I am trying to hide from Him?

When we develop a habit of hiding, we completely lose the shame signal. The Bible talks about a "seared conscience" which results from not responding continuously to the Holy Spirit's voice. 1 Timothy 4:2 (NIV) "...whose consciences have been seared as with a hot iron." To avoid developing a hardened heart we must respond to the Holy Spirit's promptings through our conscience, then obey (more later on this topic). Because we are ashamed of our shame, we hide from an emotion that God wants to use to alert us to His voice.

We need to ask ourselves, "Why am I hiding?" "Who am I hiding from?" "What am I hiding?"

Taking Ownership of Our Sin

It is interesting how God deals with Adam's problem with negative shame. God doesn't confront Adam's sin of rebellion. Instead, he asks Adam, "Who told you that you were naked? Have you eaten from the tree that I commanded you not to eat from?" (v.11) God is addressing the issue of shame. He already knows what's going on; He isn't looking for Adam to give Him an answer or an explanation.

He asks because He wants Adam to take ownership of his sin. God gives Adam an opportunity to deal with his shame. We only change in our lives that for which we acknowledge and take responsibility. When we sin against God, either knowingly or unknowingly, the only way to freedom is to confess our sin.

In Daniel 9:7–8 (NIV), in a prayer of confession, Daniel acknowledges the sin of the nation of Israel. They are being held captive in Babylon because of their unwillingness to repent for their sin of idolatry over hundreds of years (among other sins). Daniel says: "Lord, you are righteous, but this day we are covered with shame— the men of Judah and the inhabitants of Jerusalem, and all Israel, both near and far, in all the countries where you have scattered us because of our unfaithfulness to you. We and our kings, our princes and our fathers are covered with shame, Lord, because we have sinned against you."

Daniel tells us that living with unconfessed sin covers us with shame. Before the Fall, Adam was covered with the protection of innocence. After the Fall, both Adam and Eve were covered in shame. When the Holy Spirit confronts us with questions about our hearts, He wants us to acknowledge our sin to stop living in rebellion. Our confession enables God to cover us with His forgiveness and cleansing.

Notice what God does to provide a solution for Adam and Eve's sin: "And the Lord God made garments of skin for Adam and his wife and clothed them." (Genesis 3:21 NIV) An animal was sacrificed to cover Adam and Eve. This is the beginning of the story of salvation pictured for us in Scripture. God, in his mercy and kindness, not only forgives our sin and rebellion but also clothes us with His salvation. When we try to produce our own salvation, we make things worse.

Guilt and Shame Expose Sin

God uses guilt and shame signals to expose our sin so that when we repent, He clothes us in His righteousness. What a great picture! When we confess our sin, God pays the blood price for our rebellion. Adam and Eve's solution for their sin was to sew fig leaves, but God knew that only with a blood sacrifice could God's forgiveness prevail. So God sacrificed an animal to cover Adam and Eve. As we can see, this sacrifice was a prophetic foretelling of Christ on the cross that came centuries later.

The Old Testament sacrificial system was a symbolic foretelling of the need for Jesus, as the Lamb of God, to be sacrificed for all the sins of mankind. So God covered Adam and Eve with this animal sacrifice so that they wouldn't attempt to cover themselves again with fig leaves. Sacrifice was the only way they could return to relationship with God. When God provides the sacrifice, He turns negative shame into positive shame.

However, to protect Adam and Eve, God set boundaries so they could not re-enter the Garden of Eden. Exile from the Garden was the consequence of their sin, but it also was protection for them. Having eaten of the Tree of the Knowledge of Good and Evil, they were in danger of eating from the Tree of Life. Had they eaten from the Tree of Life, after already eating from the Tree of the Knowledge of Good and Evil, they would have been eternally damned. God used their shame in a positive manner by keeping Adam and Eve from destroying themselves due to their trespass. This is part of God's amazing redemptive plan.

CHAPTER 10

Shame's Relationship to Fear

Let's examine two Scripture passages to see the relationship between shame and fear. Job 11:13–15 (NIV) "Yet if you devote your heart to him and stretch out your hands to him, if you put away the sin that is in your hand and allow no evil to dwell in your tent, then you will lift up your face without shame; you will stand firm and without fear."

Interestingly, these verses are spoken by Zophar, self-righteously attempting to correct Job for his failure to see his sin. Despite the context, nevertheless Zophar spoke truth but not as he applied it to Job. When we deal properly with sin through confession, then we stand before God without negative shame and negative fear.

Jeremiah, in a prayer to God, tells us, "Let my persecutors be put to shame, but keep me from shame; let them be terrified, but keep me from terror; bring on them the day of disaster; destroy with double destruction." (Jeremiah 17:18 NIV) In this verse, Jeremiah asks God to bring judgment upon His enemies. Notice that Jeremiah equates shame with terror. Once sin has overtaken an area of our lives, we live in constant fear of exposure. We do not like to be humiliated or shamed because of our sin and failure.

As Jeremiah points out, to be exposed in a public manner is a terrifying experience. In Jeremiah 13:26 (NIV) he says that God "will pull up your skirts over your face that your shame may be seen." God is not talking here to the ladies. He is addressing men who consistently worshipped false gods. God uses shame as punishment for their unwillingness to repent for their spiritual adultery. Fear plays a large role in the outworking of shame.

The Fear of Being Found Out

When I was about eight years old, my parents bought their first television set (black and white, of course). About two years earlier, my Aunt Jessie had bought a television. Many Saturdays, my older sister, Judy, and my twin brother, Grant, and I walked to her home to watch cowboy shows (*Roy Rogers, Gene Autry, Hop Along Cassidy*, and others) on her television. I was mesmerised by television, especially because we were not allowed at that time to go to "sinful" movies in the theatre.

So when my father purchased our first television, I found every excuse to watch it. I was in grade three in school; my parents maintained that we could not watch television until our homework was done (those were the days when teachers actually gave homework to elementary children). But I was so captivated with television that I remember a number of times lying to my parents when they asked if my homework was done.

Sitting in front of the television I anticipated the show that was about to appear, simultaneously living in fear because I knew it was wrong to lie. I felt shame in what I was doing but was so addicted to watching television I ignored the shame signal. I had a sense of terror in me. I couldn't fully enjoy the show because of my shame. It was a bittersweet experience. My sin and resulting shame blocked me from enjoying what otherwise was a positive experience. Eventually, because of a tender conscience, I confessed my sin to my parents, who grounded me from watching television for a period of time.

The Fear of Being Rejected by God

Why are we so afraid with regard to shame? The answer lies in the primal experience of Adam in the Garden. Because Adam sinned against God, all human beings inherited his sin nature. Each of us fears rejection by God—one of the reasons many people are terrified of death. People intuitively know they will meet their Maker when they die. The power behind shame is the fear of rejection; no greater fear exists on earth than of rejection.

When we sin against God and try to hide, we are afraid God will punish us by rejecting us. However, when we confess our sin, God delights in forgiving and cleansing us. Somewhere in the deep recesses of our minds, we are afraid of giving an account before God for all our wrongful behaviours. Indeed, at some point, God will call all of us to give an account of our words and actions. We resist giving an account to anybody; it is part of our independence from God, which we inherited from Adam when he made a choice to be his own god.

Satan used this same temptation to deceive Eve. He said to her (my paraphrase) "Don't you want to be like God? That way you will be in control of your own life and not be under the restriction of obeying God's rules." Of course, Satan gave Eve only part of the story. This temptation of self-determination remains the single largest point of contention for all human beings. We want to rule our own lives. We don't want anyone telling us what to do and when to do it.

Shame Produces Rebellion

When we rule our own lives, we live in a place of shame because we hide from God when we "try to play God." God wants to turn our negative shame into positive shame by offering an alternative—trusting Him and submitting to His ways.

Psalm 34:4–7 (NIV) "I sought the Lord, and he answered me; he delivered me from all my fears. Those who look to him are radiant; their faces are never covered with shame." Can you recognize a shame-covered face? It's not always obvious because most of us have learned to cover our shame well. Seeing shame on "innocent" children's faces is easier because they haven't learned to hide their shame as well as have adults.

The larger challenge for us is recognizing our own face when we are caught in shame. According to Psalm 34:5, the opposite of a shame-covered face is a radiant face. Picture a child who is free and innocent with nothing to hide. A shame face is clouded, cautious, closed off, often nervous, and definitely not free.

In Psalm 34:6–7 (NIV), David says: "This poor man called, and the Lord heard him; he saved him out of all his troubles. The angel of the Lord encamps around those who fear him, and he delivers them."

When we seek the Lord, we are looking at Him face to face, like an innocent child looks at his parents.

When we are walking in openness with the Holy Spirit, God will remove not only the shame but also negative fear as well. Life without the fear of rejection is wonderful. God has forgiven all our sins, so we should never fear being rejected by God. Therefore, no sin barrier separates God from those who are forgiven and covered in Jesus' righteousness. God promises us that He will never leave us nor forsake us.

The Bible says that when we approach God with a spirit of humility or brokenness, we never have to fear rejection by Him. Psalm 51:7 (NIV) "The sacrifices of God are a broken spirit; a broken and a contrite heart, O God you will not despise."

When we hide in shame because of resulting fear, we often choose to go further into hiding. We fear being exposed or having to face our sin and failure, so we hide our sins and push them down even deeper into our unconscious. However, God tells us that we don't need to hide; He will not reject us for our weaknesses and failures. All He asks of us is to acknowledge our sin to be cleansed and then we can live freely in God's purposes. God promises that honest confession always will be heard, received, and forgiven. That's how to live in freedom every day.

CHAPTER 11

SHAME'S RELATIONSHIP
TO ANGER

Anger and shame have a lot in common. Again, we go back to the Scriptures as a basis for understanding the relationship between shame and anger. The story in 1 Samuel 20:30 (NIV) illustrates this: "Saul's anger flared up at Jonathan and he said to him, "You son of a perverse and rebellious woman! Don't I know that you have sided with the son of Jesse to your own shame and to the shame of the mother who bore you?"

In the context of this passage, Saul is angry with David because Saul was eclipsed by David's popularity—part of Saul's significant battle with insecurity. Twice Saul, in his paranoia, tries to kill David. Despite that, David gives Saul the benefit of the doubt. But now David is aware that his life is in real danger. He tells his best friend, Jonathan (Saul's son), that it isn't safe to have supper with Jonathan's father anymore. He asks Jonathan to cover for him, to make excuses as to why David will not be attending supper with the king that evening.

Jonathan tells his father that David has gone to a family sacrifice at Bethlehem. Saul's anger then shifts from David to his own son, Jonathan, and the Bible records that "Saul's anger flared up at Jonathan and he said to him, 'You son of a perverse and rebellious woman. Don't I know that you have sided with the son of Jesse, to your own shame and to the shame of the mother who bore you.'" 1 Samuel 20:30 (NIV)

We often speak foolish things in our anger. In his anger Saul criticized his own wife, and then he redirects that criticism toward his son, Jonathan. Saul tries to shame Jonathan into changing loyalties from David to himself by bringing Jonathan's mother into the dialogue. Then Saul adds even more to his shaming process: he says to Jonathan, "Because of your shame of family betrayal, you also have dragged your mother into this situation. When you side with David your friend, you also will dethrone your mother."

In other words, if Jonathan doesn't become the next king, his mother will lose her place as the queen mother. Saul is using the power of shame in a "double whammy." Not only does he shame Jonathan directly, but he attempts to manipulate Jonathan even more by putting the weight of shame on him for how he will affect his dear mother. Perhaps, when you were a child, you have had similar words spoken to you. "Do not bring shame on our family name."

Another verse in the Bible brings a commentary on the connection between shame and anger. In Jeremiah 12, God responds to Jeremiah's complaint about God's sense of justice, (Jeremiah 12:1). Jeremiah argues with God that the punishment being brought on Judah is not fair by sending them into captivity in Babylon. The wicked get away with far more, he says to God. God responds to Jeremiah that the nation of Judah has gone too far this time. "They will sow wheat but they will reap thorns. They will wear themselves out but gain nothing.

So bear the shame of your harvest because of the Lord's fierce anger." (Jeremiah 12:33, NIV)

Rebellion and Shame Bring on God's Anger

The consequence of rebellion and shame ultimately is God's anger. Many of us have experienced this in our families. When we turn against our parents we shame them. This shame, in turn, arouses our parents' anger. The consequences of unrepentant sin is disobedience and rebellion. When parents experience the overt rebellion of their children, they often express anger in return. Sound familiar?

We can see this in the story of King Saul and Jonathan that Saul is actually using his anger to cover his own shameful behaviour. Saul is living in shame and guilt. He has tried to kill David twice, even though David saved Saul's life by killing Goliath. Saul, as Israel's "giant," should have challenged Goliath on the battlefield but he was afraid. Over the next number of years, David, as a fierce warrior, won many battles against the Philistines that protected both Saul and the nation of Israel.

Because Saul is so insecure, he becomes jealous of David's popularity with the people; he tries to kill David. Saul is filled with shame for his own actions. When shame overcomes him, Saul loses control of his emotions. He uses his anger at David and Jonathan to try to regain control.

Anger is often used to cover shame. All of us perceive shame as dangerous to ourselves. We don't like shame, and we don't like feeling ashamed. It is typical to react with anger when someone tries to shame us. Interestingly, when Saul attempts to control Jonathan through shame, Jonathan does not try to shame his father in return.

However, Jonathan uses his anger to counter his father in a honourable way. The Scripture says Jonathan responded with fierce anger and left the room. Perhaps Jonathan did not want to use his fierce anger on his father, as his father just had done to him. Jonathan's response was to "get out of there" because his father's attempt to shame him had roused such indignation in Jonathan.

Using Shame as a Weapon

When we quarrel with others, we often will try to shame them. We may not be acting with conscious intent but in our anger we use shame as a weapon, just as Saul did to Jonathan. If we watch the other person carefully, we can see shame reflected in his face, particularly so in children. Yet I have seen it in adults as well.

Years ago when I was a counsellor at Lethbridge College, I was responsible for administering the California Psychological Inventory to students trying to enter the faculties of nursing, criminal justice, and the park ranger portion of the environmental science program. In those days, it was used as a screening tool to prevent students with major psychological problems from entering those programs. We did not want to admit into those programs students who were emotionally unstable. Anyone working with guns or hypodermic needles must be emotionally healthy.

I reviewed hundreds of these CPI tests, reporting any concerns to various faculty chairpersons. Occasionally I came across some concerns then shared my observations with the appropriate head of the program.

In one particular instance, an eighteen-year-old young lady was applying for the criminal justice program. I interpreted her CPI and I realized that this young lady was not psychologically fit to enter the program. If she did get in, she would only last one semester. She wasn't emotionally mature or stable enough to handle the rigors of the program. She was riddled with insecurities and could be a danger in the field. This type of negative recommendation didn't occur often, but when it did we had to act on it. After reviewing this young lady's CPI scores, I went to the head of the Criminal Justice Program and shared my concerns about allowing this student into Criminal Justice.

The chairman of the program examined some of her academic scores and realized that she was also weak on a number of other fronts. She had passed her academic tests but not by much. He called this prospective student to tell her that she was not being accepted into the program. When she questioned the chairman's decision, she was told about the additional concerns in her CPI scores. A few days later, I received an angry phone call from her mother. She was like a mother bear whose cub had been wounded and she was in a foul mood.

I invited her and her daughter to come to the counselling department to talk with me. I told her I would go over the CPI in more detail and explain my concerns to her and her daughter. As the mother walked into the office, I could sense her anger right away. I asked the daughter's permission to share with her mother the results of the test. When she agreed, I began divulging what I saw in the CPI. As I was doing this, I could tell by the daughter's reaction that I was "reading her mail" correctly. My descriptions clearly were registering with her. The mother, too, saw the descriptions as accurate.

As I was speaking, the mother suddenly shifted her anger from me onto her daughter. She poured shame and contempt on her. I understood clearly why the daughter was like she was. The mother had raised her daughter in shame, most likely because she herself had been raised in shame. The description that I was giving of her daughter was a reflection of the mother. In the mother's shame, she poured out her anger on her daughter, shaming her for not being a more successful daughter.

The daughter, in turn, had enough and began striking back at her mother with her own anger. I became the referee in this family battle. I suspected these battles were common in their home. I saw the reciprocal effect of shame and anger right before my eyes. No wonder the daughter had such scores on the CPI.

Taking on a Shame Identity

Shame doesn't always receive an active anger response in return. Sometimes, shame will produce a withdrawal response (passive anger). At other times, shame will produce a gentle, soft-spoken reaction from the other person. He simply is agreeing with the shame assessment because he has taken on a shame identity. When adults or children respond to shaming with anger, they are protecting themselves from further shame.

If you observe a child being shamed, you will see them exhibit a reaction of helplessness. Because shame is so powerful, dealing with direct anger is easier than dealing with the indirect results of shame. Similarly, when a cat is chased by a dog, normally the cat runs from the dog, unless the cat is cornered. Then the frightened cat suddenly turns into a "tiger." She becomes a vicious, clawing machine, turning the tables on the pursuing dog. In the same way, children respond with strong anger when they have been shamed too many times. Adults, too, can respond the same way after too much shaming.

Because anger can mean possible abandonment for a child (or even an adult), he may learn to internalize his anger. If a child expresses his anger to the parent or sibling and it produces more rejection or further abandonment, then the danger may cause him to repress the anger. Internalized anger can turn into fear. Internalized fear becomes anxiety. If this happens often enough, eventually the child will develop an anxiety-laden personality.

Shame and Anger Can Result in Depression

Anger continually turned inward becomes depression. Even at a young age, children can be depressed. Depression, in turn, produces a sense of self-loathing. The child begins to hate himself. If this is carried on for an extended period of time, children may attempt suicide (and, unfortunately, some succeed). In northern Canada, among some of the Inuit and aboriginal communities, suicide has become a major concern. I dare say suicide is also a concern in the rest of Canada as well.

A child who learns to hate himself will become an adult vulnerable to rejection. This self-hatred, in turn, produces rebellious teenagers who cause their parents grief during those tumultuous adolescent years of finding independence. When we don't recognize the cycles of shame and anger in children to cut them off, we produce painful family situations. In fact, as I am writing this manuscript, I am aware that some readers will recognize the pattern from your own adolescent years, or from your present family situation.

Allow me to interrupt what you are reading to pray for you so that the enemy does not use this material in a self-destructive manner by further shaming you.

Father, Your truth does cut to the quick but your truth was never designed to destroy. Your truth is designed to bring freedom. I'm asking at this moment that You would not allow our enemy, Satan, to turn this revelation of shame and anger into condemnation or accusation. Instead, I am asking that it will lead to greater desire to continue to journey toward freedom. I pray for an angelic protection over those who are reading this material so they can find a place of security and rest in You. Bring further illumination to the readers that will assist in their journey of freedom and wholeness. Amen.

CHAPTER 12

SHAME'S RELATIONSHIP TO REJECTION AND INSECURITY

When Adam and Eve sinned against God in the Garden of Eden, they tried to hide themselves from God because they rightly feared His rejection. Once they disobeyed God, the guilt signal alerted them that something was wrong. Because they didn't know how to deal with the guilt signal (as it was the first time to experience it) they immediately looked for a place to hide. Theirs was the first expression of shame.

Whenever we are hurt or rejected by someone, we feel insecure; this insecurity is a form of shame. (Insecurity is also related to fear. Insecurity is a state of living in negative fear.) When we have unresolved shame in our past, we are vulnerable to people's derisive comments. Such comments are like a heat-seeking missile, always landing in our hearts. It is possible the enemy knows these areas of vulnerability in our lives so he can target most effectively for maximum pain.

Getting the Goats Out

Years ago, I attended a seminar led by a Catholic nun. Although diminutive in size, what she lacked in stature she made up through a powerful message. The one takeaway I remember from that seminar was: "Nobody can get your goat, unless there is a goat in there to get." (If I could remember her name I would give her credit for her statement, but I have no recollection of her name.) Nevertheless, I have used that quote numerous times and everybody understands.

When we have unresolved "goats" in our past and people express something to us that approximates that "goat," we hide in shame. We need to acknowledge such a "goat" in us and move towards getting the "goat" out through receiving healing. How do we know when this heat-seeking missile has hit? Our eyes well up with tears, we can feel it in our emotions, in the flush of our face, a lump in our throat, or the tension in our body.

When we become aware that something has hit the target, we look for a place to hide. But what we need to do is acknowledge that there is a "goat" in our lives that needs to be expunged. If the target is removed then that missile can't hit it anymore. If someone speaks the truth to us, we need to deal with it—not hide from it. Otherwise, shame rules our lives in that area. If what was said exposes a "lie" in us, then let's deal with the lie through repentance.

All of us carry lies spoken into our lives in childhood. Part of the journey of sanctification for the Christian is finding those lies and replacing them with the truth from God's Word. Many of the lies we believe about ourselves are not located in our minds but in our emotions. That is why we react to unkind words spoken to us. The impact is that much greater when the lie has an emotional root.

Unexamined Shame Wounds

The more insecure we feel about ourselves, the more self-doubts we have, the more likely we are to interpret a comment as rejection. This usually means we have unexamined shame wounds. There is a strong correlation between shame wounds and deep insecurity. The more shame that remains, the more people have control over us. The more insecure we feel, the greater the shame we live in. Many people experience this vicious cycle regularly.

One of the main reasons I am writing this book is to expose the lies and insecurities in our lives, so that we can make a conscious choice to deal with them. However, we cannot guarantee that once shame has been exposed, we will deal with it. We intentionally must go after the shame. If you don't know the hidden areas of the heart, you never can make a choice to work it through. Therefore, Satan likes to keep these issues hidden. In fact, we actually have been trained to hide many things. We learned from our grandparents, Adam and Eve, to hide.

Even when proper correction is given to a child by his parents, the child can receive it wrongly. Why? Because a lie has already formed in the child's life; the child is reacting to that lie. I'm sure parents know exactly what I am expressing. When your child struggles with a particular area of insecurity, your correction is for his good but he can't receive it. He feels you are attacking his self-esteem. This especially may be the case when you are dealing with adopted children (for whom the lie of abandonment and rejection is strong) or dealing with foster children who are wards of the government.

The correction is received as rejection, because the child is carrying so much shame from the past. 1 Corinthians 4:14 (NIV) illustrates this issue. Paul, recognizing the danger of correction being taken wrongly, wants to address an issue with the Corinthian church. In the process of bringing correction to them he says: "I am not writing this to shame you, but to warn you, as my dear children." Paul obviously sensed that some of the people in the Corinthian church were in danger of misinterpreting the correction he was bringing for their good. They would receive this correction as shame rather than corrective help.

Shame Expects Rejection

To live in shame is to expect rejection, not because of what we have done but because of what we believe about ourselves. If we live in insecurity, we believe we are worthy of the derisive comments given to us. When someone speaks them to us, we receive them because of what we already believe about ourselves.

On the one hand, we don't want to believe these lies; we want to hear affirming compliments. On the other hand, when the lie is already formed in our psyches, we receive the damaging criticism because that's whom we believe we are. However, when shame is brought to the light, we are on the way to confronting this lie hidden in our souls. To be emotionally healthy people, we must remove those hidden areas of the heart.

Negative shame means not being good enough. This poor self-concept keeps people on the "treadmill" of performance, trying to please others for acceptance. The only way off this "treadmill" is to acknowledge that no one is ever good enough; that is why we need God's forgiveness. That's the joy of the gospel message. We are not good enough but Jesus is. He is perfect and we are not. That's why His death on the cross was sufficient to be "good enough" (read perfect) for us when we believe the message of the Gospel.

We not only have to believe this truth but also we must personally receive this good news. People often reject God because they don't feel good enough. The whole point of the gospel message is: nobody is good enough. Paul stated clearly in Roman 3:10–12 (NIV): "As it is written: 'There is no one righteous, not even one; there is no one who understands, no one who seeks God. All have turned away, they have together become worthless; there is no one who does good, not even one.'"

Ashamed of Deficits and Assets

In our state of insecurity, we not only are ashamed of what we dislike about ourselves but also we are ashamed of what we like about ourselves. We not only are ashamed of our deficits but also our assets. We even become ashamed of our creativity; in some cases, our genius. Why? Because we see ourselves as different; this is not acceptable because of our insecurity. Many of us find our acceptance and security from being the same as others.

I remember counselling a young man at Lethbridge College. He was referred to me by one of the instructors. He told me that this student was a conundrum. In the previous semester he was at the top of his class in electronics. But since returning from the Christmas break, he failed all his exams.

I agreed to meet with this student to see if I could understand what was going on. I wondered what would cause this dramatic change from one semester to the next. Because he was an insecure young man, I worked at getting him to be open. I asked him about his family and how was his Christmas vacation. I asked about his father and what line of work he was in. He told me his father was a farmer and that he had grown up in a farming community. I asked him what his father thought of his college training in the electronics program. He replied, "Not much."

Did his father know how well he had done in his first semester? Yes, he had shared his success with his family when he was home at Christmas. He told them proudly that he had A's in every class. As he told me this, I noticed his eyes watering. He told me that his father had neither interest nor respect for the field of electronics. Because his father had no understanding of modern technology, it threatened him. He was an "old school" farmer who had no use for the latest innovations in electronics.

Then I began to understand. This student had tremendous ability in a field that his father failed to understand and appreciate. When his father rejected his son's assets the student also rejected them, because he desperately wanted his father's acceptance. I asked him if he was angry with his father. He said he wasn't. Because it was clear he loved his father very much, he made a choice to reject himself in order to keep his father's acceptance. I dared to challenge his thinking. I said, "You really are angry at your father because he won't affirm what you are good at and what you hope to become."

Finally he acknowledged this anger but he continued to express how much he loved his father. He allowed me to work through his forgiveness for his father. I assured him that his father did not need to know what we worked through. This student's forgiveness of his father was enough. We also worked through the shame he felt about his father's inability to join the twentieth century. This young man was ashamed of who he was because his assets were being rejected by his father.

He knew he would continue dealing with the tension of wanting his father's love, yet also fulfilling his natural gifts. His difficulty was accepting himself in this career choice while still wanting to receive his father's acceptance. Many people mistakenly think that if their assets divide them from others, making them too different, they must dismiss their assets rather than risk being rejected.

An Ugly Self-Portrait

Behind the locked door of shame in our lives often lies an ugly self-portrait that we ourselves have painted, some of which is real, some of which is false perception. As we now understand, a great deal comes from lies that we believed about ourselves from childhood.

One of the early ways that I personally sought to overcome my insecurity was to increasingly order and structure my life. As long as I had structure, I could have a modicum of security (or so I thought). Years later in my adult life, someone once complimented me on my organizational and administrative abilities. I could not receive that compliment because I was aware of the origins of my administrative ability. My strength in administrative ability developed as a means of coping with my insecurity, for which I was still carrying shame.

On the one hand, it was true that this ability developed as a compensation for my insecurity. On the other hand, I became good at administration and organizing my life (and other's lives too). It aided me in my church work, my counselling, my ability as a teacher at the college, and in my home life. But I discovered I rejected this asset because I felt ashamed of how it developed in my life through compensating for my insecurities.

One day a friend of mine recognized this shame in me and asked my why I was ashamed to acknowledge my obvious administrative ability. He said to me, "That's a quality a lot of us wished we had, Graham." I since have corrected this perception; that is why I can write about it.

We often can't understand the issues behind the "door" of shame because the fear of rejection (which is the power behind shame) is so powerful we don't dare to open that "door." Therefore, the cycle of more insecurity and more rejection continues, which further convinces us to keep the shame "door" locked.

Take a Look in Your Closet of Shame

I want to encourage you to look behind the "locked door" of shame. Some of you reading right now never even knew of a closet of shame in your life. That's how effective the enemy has kept it hidden. Even when we realize shame in our emotions, we struggle with what to do. We may think: *No way am I opening that door to anyone, let alone admit it to myself.* Some of us have made silent (unconscious) vows that we will never let anyone into those areas of shame.

Here is a question: how can the Holy Spirit help you work through those hidden shame issues if you won't let Him in? Wherever we have unresolved issues of shame, guilt, fear, or bitterness, we are a prisoner to our pasts. I believe all people long for freedom. Most Christians want to be used by God in His Kingdom purposes. I am aware of this desire from my own story. When I was beginning to open my heart in faith to Kingdom expansion, Satan threatened to expose my unresolved shame issues. The fear of having that "closet door" opened caused me to pull back. I vowed I would never allow myself to be so vulnerable. I will share more later in the book.

In order to live in the freedom for which Jesus died, we have to work on these unresolved issues. Therefore, we also must touch the areas of unresolved guilt in our lives, not just shame. So next I will show you what the Bible teaches about guilt. These two concepts, guilt and shame, combine to keep us from freedom. But guilt is different from shame, as we will see.

CHAPTER 13

SHAME'S RELATIONSHIP
TO GUILT

Let's begin this section by examining Scripture verses about guilt and shame. Ezra Chapter 9 is the first passage. Here's the background.

The Jewish people have returned from seventy years of captivity in Babylon. On their return to the land of Israel, God commanded them to rebuild the temple of God and, eventually, the city walls of Jerusalem. In the midst of this return to their own country, Ezra discovers blatant sin tolerated by the returnees. The largest issue was the intermarriage of the Jewish people with the locals. This is one of the sins (of the many) that sent the nation of Israel into captivity in the first place. Intermarriage caused many of the Jewish people to worship other gods than Yahweh.

Ezra 9:5–9; 13–15 (NIV):

5   "Then, at the evening sacrifice, I rose from my self-abasement, with my tunic and cloak torn, and fell on my knees with my hands spread out to the Lord my God

6   and prayed: "I am too ashamed and disgraced, my God, to lift up my face to you, because our sins are higher than our heads and our guilt has reached to the heavens.

7   From the days of our ancestors until now, our guilt has been great. Because of our sins, we and our kings and our priests have been subjected to the sword and captivity, to pillage and humiliation at the hand of foreign kings, as it is today.

8   "But now, for a brief moment, the Lord our God has been gracious in leaving us a remnant and giving us a firm place in his sanctuary, and so our God gives light to our eyes and a little relief in our bondage.

9   Though we are slaves, our God has not forsaken us in our bondage. He has shown us kindness in the sight of the kings of Persia: He has granted us new life to rebuild the house of our God and repair its ruins, and he has given us a wall of protection in Judah and Jerusalem."

13   "What has happened to us is a result of our evil deeds and our great guilt, and yet, our God, you have punished us less than our sins deserved and have given us a remnant like this.

14   Shall we then break your commands again and intermarry with the peoples who commit such detestable practices?

Would you not be angry enough with us to destroy us,
leaving us no remnant or survivor?

15 Lord, the God of Israel, you are righteous! We are left
this day as a remnant. Here we are before you in our
guilt, though because of it not one of us can stand in your
presence."

Confessing Sin

Another passage from the Bible we want to examine is Psalm 32, written by King David. Over David's lifetime, he grappled with various sins
and mistakes (just like us). However, David never allowed these sins
to take over his life for long. He learned to confess his sin and deal
with his guilt so it didn't turn into shame. **Psalm 32:1–5 (NIV)** is an
example of this.

1   Blessed is the one
whose transgressions are forgiven,
whose sins are covered.

2   Blessed is the one
whose sin the Lord does not count against them
and in whose spirit is no deceit.

3   When I kept silent,
my bones wasted away
through my groaning all day long.

4   For day and night
your hand was heavy on me;
my strength was sapped

as in the heat of summer.
5 Then I acknowledged my sin to you
and did not cover up my iniquity.
I said, "I will confess
my transgressions to the Lord."
And you forgave
the guilt of my sin.

Both of the above passages of Scripture give us some understanding of the power of guilt. Ezra tears his clothes and prostrates himself before God. Have you ever experienced the guilt of your sin having such a powerful impact on you? Ezra said that he was so ashamed of the guilt of his people that he could hardly look up to heaven. Psalm 32 is David's clear description of guilt and the effects of it on our body and soul. David had experienced this impact of guilt on his life; he knew firsthand what he was writing. David describes the pressure of guilt upon him as one completely sapped of energy. It robbed him of his ability to live a healthy life, both emotionally and physically.

Objective Guilt

In Appendix 3, I have inserted a diagram to give an overview of guilt and how it impacts us. Guilt is the fact or state of breaking a divine or human law, which, in turn, carries the appropriate penalty for such violation. There are two types of guilt in Scripture. The first, objective guilt, arises where a law has been broken and the lawbreaker is held responsible—even though he or she may not **feel** guilty. In many instances in which a person has broken the law, he may not feel guilt.

Why? Possibly, because his conscience is seared. In other instances, he may not realize he has broken the law. It doesn't matter how he feels. Nevertheless he is guilty because he has transgressed the law of God or the law of the land.

For example: You are driving your car on the highway at the posted speed, but you have not noticed that the speed limit has just changed to a lower speed. When the officer pulls you over, you protest that you didn't see the sign showing the speed limit was lowered. He says to you, "Ignorance of the law is no excuse." He gives you a ticket because you broke the law. In other circumstances, the person driving his car doesn't care about what the posted limit is. He drives at whatever speed he chooses. He, too, is guilty even when he doesn't feel guilty. In this case, he falsely thinks he is above the law.

Responses to Dealing with Guilt

According to the Bible, three responses are necessary to deal properly with objective guilt. When we have sinned and are guilty, we must first seek forgiveness from God. In Psalm 51, David confesses his sin of adultery with Bathsheba and his sin of murdering Uriah, her husband. Notice, however, that he states: "against You, and You only, have I sinned" (Psalm 51:4 NIV). All sin is first and foremost against God.

But also we need to deal with the guilt of sinning against one another. In Matthew 5:23–24, Jesus says that if we know we have sinned against someone, we should leave what we are doing (even if we are at church worshipping) and go to make it right with our brother or sister. Jesus describes it as serious business. Seeking forgiveness from the person we have wronged is the key first step in dealing with guilt.

The next step in getting released from our guilt is to repent for the sin we have committed. Repentance is changing our minds, or our thinking. Repentance is only possible when we get God's perspective on our sin. Many Christians think that repentance means to change one's behaviour. Changing behaviour is only possible by first changing one's thinking. A change of behaviour follows a change of thinking. Our minds first must recognize that we have sinned.

In Acts 26:19 (NIV), as Paul is testifying before King Agrippa in Caesarea, he says: "I was not disobedient to the vision from heaven. First to those in Damascus, and then those in Jerusalem and in all Judea, and to the Gentiles also, I preached that they should repent and turn to God and prove their repentance by their deeds." Notice Paul's comment: we prove our repentance by our behaviour or deeds.

The Scriptures clearly define repentance as a change of mind, which causes a change of behaviour. Without a change in our thinking processes, a change of behaviour will be superficial or short-lived. The Greek word for *repentance* in the New Testament (*metanoeo*) literally means to change the mind. When God shows us through the guilt signal that we have sinned against Him, we repent. We are saying in our repentance, "You are right, God, I am wrong and now I am shifting my thinking and behaviour to line up with your thinking."

When we have repented and received forgiveness, we need to follow up. This is called restitution. Where we have wronged God or another human being by stealing from them, part of our repentance is to restore the money to our victim. Once I talked with a man who was angry at God, angry at his pastor, and angry at his church. As a result, he refused to tithe. After years of being a faithful tither, his anger justified his right to quit tithing. Several years later he realized he was wrong and he repented. He then began systematically to pay back his tithe of several thousand dollars month by month by month. This payback was his restitution to God (and his church).

Zacchaeus, in the New Testament, is an example of this principle of restitution. Having found relationship with Jesus, he made a promise to pay back what he had wrongfully taken in his tax collection business. He not only made restitution but he made it fourfold. His reimbursement was a result of true repentance. When we have broken the law of God, or the state, the Biblical pattern is first to repent then receive God's forgiveness and, finally, make restitution where warranted.

Subjective Guilt

Scripture also presents a second type of guilt, which I refer to as subjective guilt. Subjective guilt means **feelings** of guilt. Subjective guilt functions as an emotional signal, telling us to listen to that "inner voice" and examine our hearts. Subjective guilt is the internal feelings of correction, remorse, or self-condemnation that can result from right or wrong perceptions of our own behaviour. In other words, when we feel guilty, we need to examine whether the guilt is true or false guilt.

When we feel guilty, we check out the guilt signal to see if we have wronged God or someone else. Sometimes we may be "feeling" guilty but in fact we have not wronged anyone. When people tell me they feel guilty, I say to them, "Let's examine this guilt signal." The one thing we don't want to do is to ignore this signal. We need to find out what the guilt is telling us. Unresolved guilt (whether true or false) turns into shame. When it becomes shame, then it is hidden from us. Remember that true guilt is given to us to aid us in seeing when we are living in disobedience to God's commands. Obviously, if a Christian violates God's righteousness, he needs to get back on track.

True Guilt is Our Friend

Guilt is our friend, not our enemy. However, Satan always is trying to use guilt against us. If we don't understand the difference between true guilt and false guilt, we will be vulnerable to accusations of guilt. True guilt always is a signal from the Holy Spirit, telling us something is wrong. True guilt always arises from a specific act that needs to be corrected. The basis for right and wrong is always the word of God, not someone else's opinion of right and wrong. In all true guilt, we can make a corrective change. True guilt then will take us to seek forgiveness, repentance, and possible restitution.

False guilt often fools us because the enemy (and others who use false guilt) will use the power of guilt against us. False guilt is manipulation. Moreover, false guilt is the same as witchcraft. Guilt, like shame, is a powerful emotion. People with low self-esteem or people with a strong need to please are especially vulnerable to false guilt. When other people attempt to get us to do what they want, they use false guilt to manipulate us.

False guilt causes anger in us because, sooner or later, we realize we have been deceived. We react with anger because manipulation is danger to us. We do not like being tricked with false guilt. At times false guilt will cause us to feel condemned, because we are fed a lie. Other times we respond with what the Bible calls "worldly sorrow"— this leads us nowhere. In 2 Corinthians 7:8–10 (NIV), Paul comments:

"Even if I caused you sorrow by my letter, I do not regret it. Though I did regret it—I see that my letter hurt you, but only for a little while—yet now I am happy, not because you were made sorry, but because your sorrow led you to repentance. For you became sorrowful as God intended and so were not harmed in any way by us. Godly sorrow brings repentance that leads to salvation and leaves no regret, but worldly sorrow brings death."

The Sources of Power on Earth

Only two sources of power exist on the earth— God's and Satan's (and Satan's power is usurped from God). God's power is called grace. Satan's power is called witchcraft. When we use God's power to bring about changes in the Kingdom of God, we must remain in line with God's righteousness and His purposes. Using Satan's power of manipulation to bring about Kingdom purposes is a terrifying transgression. I have seen this witchcraft operating on a few occasions when churches need money to advance what they believe is a Kingdom goal. Using manipulation to bring in resources is wrong even when the goal is right.

Many falsely believe a third source of power exists called the power of the flesh, but in reality, the power of the flesh is empowered by the enemy. When we pressure people into doing what we want them to do, we are using the power of the flesh (manipulation) to accomplish our purposes. Sometimes we use manipulation in raising our children but without realization. The goal of children's obedience to parents is correct, but we can't use the enemy's tactics to accomplish this goal. As much as we want to see people become Christians, we cannot use manipulation to convince them of the reality of Christ. I have seen situations where this false guilt is used shamelessly without people realizing it.

I am aware that at times I have used this false guilt myself. When I rethink my parenting years, I am made aware of the number of times I used false guilt inadvertently. I, too, was raised with some false guilt, yet my parents would be dismayed if they knew they had used it. After I began to understand false guilt, I told our teenaged children, "If you ever sense I'm using false guilt on you, tell me." And believe me they did catch me, as did my wife, Sherry.

I'm thankful I told my children because I became aware of unconsciously using false guilt. A common expression I hear parents say is: "If you really love me, you will do this for me." That's manipulation; instead, we ought to ask our children to obey us without putting on a condition of love. "Just do it because I ask you to do it." Here's another one: "I did all this work for you and that's all I get in return." Ouch!

CHAPTER 14

COMPARING SHAME AND GUILT

Shame and guilt are similar in some ways; therefore, many people confuse these concepts. Shame is an emotion similar to what we call guilt feelings, but they are not the same. Guilt feelings function as signals to tell us that our behaviour has slipped off the "straight and narrow." Shame also functions as a signal to tell us that something is wrong. Something has been hidden in our lives that needs to be exposed. As such, shame and guilt are similar.

However, guilt is uniquely different from shame. **Guilt refers to what we have done, whereas shame becomes a perception of who we are.** When we do something wrong and are aware that we need to change—that is guilt working. When you conclude that you are a terrible person because of what you have done, that is shame functioning. Shame falsely communicates that you are hopeless, which causes you to give up making changes in your lives.

Thus, our enemy, Satan, catches us repeatedly. Instead of using the guilt signal to expose our sin and failure, we repress the guilt and hide it in our "shame closet." Objective guilt alerts us that we are breaking the laws of God (and man) even when we don't feel guilty. Deep within every human being, regardless of religious background, lies a sense that not all is right. We know we have a debt that needs to be repaid. This sense of debt motivates people in the religions of the world to try harder. They think maybe, somehow, they can make atonement for their sin. Let's explore this idea more fully.

Dealing with False Guilt

In North American and in European societies in particular, trying to avoid any sense of guilt doesn't make guilt disappear. Satan will attempt to duplicate everything that God uses for our good and turn it around for our destruction. False guilt tries to make us feel badly for something we can't correct. We feel guilty, but we don't know how to handle the "guilt" because it's not true. True guilt always gives us something to rework. Whenever someone in counselling says, "I'm feeling guilty. I don't know what to do," I immediately ask him if the guilt he is feeling lines up with the word of God. If it does, he can correct it through confession and repentance.

A lot of our accumulated false guilt turns into shame, because we don't know how to work through it. On the other hand, when we don't deal properly with true guilt, we are much more vulnerable to being fooled by false guilt later. Not working through the lie associated with false guilt leaves us vulnerable to be tricked by Satan. He doesn't want us dealing with our true guilt. Let me give you an example.

When parents use false guilt to manipulate their children to obey, the children may comply but they will carry internal resentment toward their parents. They will sense (maybe subconsciously) they have been manipulated into obeying even when they are not aware right away. Later, when the children disobey again and the parents attempt to correct the children by asking them to deal with their wrong correctly, the children will become confused. To protect themselves from possible manipulation, they will not want to acknowledge what they have done wrong.

Totally Forgiven

Most Christians are aware that when a person is born again, all their sins are forgiven—past, present, and future. The theological term is called *justification*. The newly born Christian is forgiven once for all. However, having been justified or completely forgiven does not mean that the Christian is cleansed from unrighteousness or ongoing sin in his life. This is the process of sanctification, which goes on for as long as we are on this side of heaven.

Hebrews 10:11–14 (NIV) makes this point clear. "Day after day every priest stands and performs his religious duties; again and again he offers the same sacrifices, which can never take away sins. But when this priest had offered for all time one sacrifice for sins, he sat down at the right hand of God, and since that time he waits for his enemies to be made his footstool. For by one sacrifice he has made perfect forever those who are being made holy."

The answer for ongoing sin in our lives is confession and cleansing. 1 John 1:9 (NIV) clarifies: "If we confess our sins, he is faithful and just and will forgive us our sins and purify us from all unrighteousness." The Greek word for *purify* (*katharizo*—from which we get our English word *catharsis*) is the same word used in Luke for the cleansing of a leper. When we don't deal with confession and cleansing regularly, we are much more vulnerable to being fooled by the enemy with false guilt. This is the reason why it is so important to confess our daily sins regularly.

When false guilt is not resolved, it automatically is repressed into shame. When we don't know we are being manipulated by false guilt, we cannot deal with it. However, when we recognize false guilt, we can refute it by seeing the lie behind it and challenging that lie with the truth of God's Word. Because we often don't recognize false guilt (especially when used on us frequently), we have no way of dealing with it; by default it will be repressed into shame.

This shame makes us feel unacceptable to God and others (even those who love us); we know no way to correct this unacceptability. Many of you reading this book will identify these points. We feel so badly about ourselves that we don't know how to come to God with our confession to seek His cleansing.

Feeling Trapped

We become trapped in this false state of unacceptability. God has provided a way out of this mess but because we are caught in shame, we see no way out. Ezra points out in the passage quoted earlier that our shame can be so great that we don't know how to approach God.

Shame is difficult to separate from guilt, because unresolved guilt can trigger shame; accordingly the shame that we identify with can cause false guilt. So guilt complicates shame and shame complicates resolving guilt. These links make dealing with our guilt and shame very confusing and difficult. Let's see if we can make this complicated situation clearer so we don't give Satan room to fool us.

As I said earlier, guilt refers to behaviour, whereas shame connects with our identity. Psalm 119:31–32 (NIV) says, "I hold fast to your statutes, O Lord. Do not let me be put to shame. I run in the path of your commands for you have set my heart free." If we want to keep ourselves from falling into shame, we must know God's truth and then obey it. Psalm 119:80 (NIV) says, "May my heart be blameless toward your decrees that I am not put to shame." Shame has no place in our lives when we are obeying what the Holy Spirit directs through God's Word.

The Holy Spirit corrects us through the guilt signal. We bring our guilt to God in confession and then receive His cleansing. Then we don't need to hide anymore. When we stay in the presence of God, our faces shine from being in His glory and there is no shame in us.

Dealing with Grief

People who are deeply ashamed of a particular emotion, as they often are with fear, anger, guilt, insecurity or grief, do not have access to these emotional signals. The issues these emotions are signalling remain unresolved. One of the emotions that creates confusion for us is grief. Grief is a form of anger because grief refers to loss, and loss is danger to us. Anger is the energy in us that God has given us to deal with danger. When we lose someone dear to us, we are angry at the loss because of its danger to us. To resolve grief, we have to get the anger or grief out of our emotional systems. We do that by crying, talking, reminiscing, sharing pain, discussing the loved one we lost, or other means.

Once, in counselling session, a young man told me that when he was four years old, both parents were killed in a car accident. One of the extended family members made a decision that this four-year-old was too young to understand what was going on in the funeral service, so he did not attend his parents' funerals. For years this young man had unresolved anger and did not know why. All this grief and anger was still in him. Now that he was an adult, he did not know why he constantly reacted in anger to many issues.

In another story from parents I was counselling who were new immigrants to Canada, the pregnant mother had a stillborn baby. The baby was disposed of by the hospital without any funeral or opportunity to grieve. Because the father didn't speak much English at the time, he didn't know how to challenge the decision made by the hospital.

Twenty years later, the mother was dealing with some ongoing, unknown anger toward her husband without knowing why she was so angry despite her husband loving her so much. When I probed into their past, this story of their stillborn child was shared. Both the parents were carrying hidden shame that they could not identify, which came out in forms of anger and tension in their relationship.

Because Sherry and I had also experienced the loss of a stillborn baby, we were able to minister effectively to both of them, particularly the mother. The mother expressed her grief and false guilt (she had done nothing wrong) to us; accordingly we helped her work through her latent grief. We also prompted the husband to ask forgiveness from his wife for his confusion in not knowing how to deal with it at the time. It was a life-changing experience for this couple. They were so grateful to know that hidden shame was operating in them. They believed their shame primarily arose from being new immigrants to Canada, not having a good grasp of the English language nor the Canadian culture.

Shame Inhibits Emotional Signals

When we live in constant shame yet don't know why, shame will inhibit the discharge of the emotions within. We lose the purpose of the emotional signal designed to help us deal with pain and sin in our lives. **Remember, these emotions are given to us by God to signal us that something needs to be addressed.** The locked door of shame prevents us from using our emotions for their God-given purpose. Negative shame has power over us when we continue to believe the lie that hiding from God is all we can do.

So many people I have met over the years live in shame because they don't know how to work out their shame issues. This shame also blocks many other emotional signals. How many reading this book know you have repressed certain emotions because you didn't know how to deal with them? Instead of accepting Jesus' punishment on the cross (which satisfied Father God's anger at our sin), we punish ourselves through shame. We go into hiding and withdraw from others, or we beat up ourselves and turn this unresolved guilt into self-pity (which is really a form or pride).

God's simple and effective solution is to confess our sins, receive Jesus' cleansing, and step back into God's plan for right living. I know it can often seem complicated because of the backlog of sin and unbelief that needs to be dealt with, but we can work through it all. When we submit to God's strategy for working things out, we can receive our forgiveness and healing, moving back into God's plans for daily living. God says in Psalm 51 that He will never despise a contrite heart, no matter how many times in the day you come to Him with your confessions. With true confession and repentance, we never fear rejection by God.

CHAPTER 15

God's Purpose for Emotions

God created us with emotions for three reasons. Our emotions enable us to experience life as God intended us to experience it. Without emotions, we would all be like the fictitious Mr. Spock on the television series, *Star Trek*. Apparently because he was from the planet Vulcan, he was not endowed with any emotions. His intellect was overdeveloped, but he was an emotional midget. Many wounded people on this planet look like they were teleported from the planet Vulcan. We were given emotions by God so we could experience life fully. That experience on planet earth includes the negative emotions of fear, insecurity, and anger as well as the positive emotions of joy, compassion, and happiness.

Secondly, emotions are the energy of the soul. Just as physical energy is necessary for doing physical work or play, so emotional energy is necessary for the activities of the soul. Students studying in college or university sometimes complain that they are unable to concentrate in preparing for an exam. The reason for their lack of concentration is because of limited emotional energy.

I worked in the counselling department at Lethbridge College for a number of years. I discovered that students frequently wrestled with issues in their lives such as finances, relationship problems, tensions at home or in their dormitories. All of their emotional energy was used up solving their daily life problems, leaving no emotional energy for concentrating on their studies.

Emotional energy is necessary for dealing with daily decisions, thinking about problems, conversing with others, reading, and a host of other mental, emotional, and volitional issues. Without emotional energy, people have limited desire and ability even to get out of bed in the morning. Emotional energy provides us with the "zip" that makes life interesting and enjoyable.

Emotions Are an Early Warning System

Thirdly, emotions function as signals, to act as an early warning system. These signals enable our minds to "sense" that something is happening before we have had time to think it through clearly. **Mark 5** [29] (NIV): "Immediately her bleeding stopped and she **felt** in her body that she was freed from her suffering" (my emphasis). **Jude 1** [3] (NIV): "Dear friends, although I was very eager to write to you about the salvation we share, I **felt** I had to write and urge you to contend for the faith that was once for all entrusted to the saints" (my emphasis). This woman, who was healed by Jesus, was alerted in her emotions before her mind had time to process what was happening. In Jude's case, he had a sense from his emotions that he needed to write to his fellow Christians, urging them "to contend for the faith." The emotional signal in him caused him to follow through with a letter to them.

However, the joy of having emotions is also fraught with the danger of being wrongly led or manipulated by our emotions. Nevertheless, to be "emotionless" is of no greater value than to be "emotional." Emotions need to function as God intended. Since emotions are designed by God as signals to warn persons of possible dangers, emotions must be taken seriously as clues but not as truth. The truth needs to be ascertained by the mind with the aid of a human spirit that is in contact with the Holy Spirit, who is the communicator of God's absolute truth. When the truth has been clarified by the mind and spirit, the will must engage to do what God has revealed as right and good.

When your emotions get locked behind the "door of shame" and you fail to respond to those signals, you are not able to function fully in how God has created you to operate. Quite frankly, all of us, in one form or another, are living in a blunted fashion because of unresolved issues of shame. Earlier, I encouraged you to pray and give the Lord permission to start acknowledging those things you have been afraid to touch.

Now I again want to challenge you to take another step forward. As you already have done, I'm asking you to open the "door of shame" another crack and allow the Holy Spirit to touch one area that you previously have been unable to examine. You will need to move gently because opening "the door of shame" is fearful. I know that from experience because I have done it several times. Here is your challenge:

Take a few moments to pray asking God to show you any areas in your emotions that need freedom from hidden areas of shame. If you hear something from the Holy Spirit, write down what He has shown you and ask Him to make a way for the healing to come.

Holy Spirit, help us now as we listen to You. I ask you, Father, to guard us against the enemy's accusations. When we dare to open the door of shame, keep us from anything that will be harmful to us. Lord Jesus, enable us as we pray to sense your comfort, security, courage, and presence as we open our hearts. Helps us to deal honestly with those things in our hearts you want healed. In Jesus' name, Amen.

CHAPTER 16

JESUS AND A CLEAR CONSCIENCE

1 Peter 5:8 (NIV) says to "be self controlled and alert. Your enemy the devil prowls around like a roaring lion looking for someone to devour." If you knew that someone was prowling around your neighbourhood, would you be aware of the need to be a little more vigilant? I think the correct answer is YES!

Many years ago, we had a "Peeping Tom" poking around our neighbourhood. The police told us to be on the alert. They asked us to keep our basement bedroom windows covered and to keep an eye out for this pervert on the prowl. Of course, the neighbours all were feeling unnerved by this news. Eventually (unfortunately), an eighteen-year-old son of one of the neighbours was caught. While the neighbours were relieved, we all felt badly for the tough time one of our neighbours was going through to work out this indiscretion with their son.

Satan's Weapons

We all need to watch for the traps that the enemy sets. The devil's attacks are fairly stereotypical throughout the ages, yet he relies on the fact that we ignore his patterns. In other words, we are not very vigilant. Satan's principal weapons are deception, accusation, and blackmail (intimidation), as stated in Revelation 12: 7–12 (NIV).

7 And there was war in heaven. Michael and his angels fought against the dragon, and the dragon and his angels fought back.

8 But he was not strong enough, and they lost their place in heaven.

9 The great dragon was hurled down—that ancient serpent called the devil, or Satan, who leads the whole world astray. He was hurled to the earth, and his angels with him.

10 Then I heard a loud voice in heaven say:
   "Now have come the salvation and the power
   and the kingdom of our God,
   and the authority of his Christ.
   For the accuser of our brothers,
   who accuses them before our God day and night,
   has been hurled down.

11 They overcame him
   by the blood of the Lamb
   and by the word of their testimony;
   they did not love their lives so much
   as to shrink from death.

12 Therefore rejoice, you heavens

and you who dwell in them!
But woe to the earth and the sea,
because the devil has gone down to you!
He is filled with fury,
because he knows that his time is short."

One of the areas Satan consistently uses to deceive us is disputing our freedom in Christ through our forgiveness. He lies to us, accuses us, and then blackmails us with false guilt and shame. We know we are forgiven, but we often **do not live** as if we were forgiven. Satan's goal is to keep us in darkness and shame. His strategy is to distort or restrict our knowledge of God. He wants our knowledge of God to be either erroneous or inadequate, so we will turn away from God rather than turning to Him. Satan uses condemnation, shame, and false guilt to rob us of our freedom in Jesus. Because we do not understand the power of the blood of Christ to totally cleanse us of our sin, we slide back into shame.

Hebrews 9:14 (NIV) expresses a major truth that counteracts this deception from the enemy.

"How much more, then, will the blood of Christ, who through the eternal Spirit offered himself unblemished to God, cleanse our consciences from acts that lead to death, so that we may serve the living God!" (I recommend reading the whole of Hebrews 9 in *The Message Bible* to get a greater sense of the context of verse 14).

Review of Hebrews 9

Let's do a quick review of Hebrews chapter 9 to capture the context of verse 14. The first six verses describe the Old Testament tabernacle, the Holy of Holies, and the system that was used to deal with people who had sinned in that era. In verses 7 and 8 of Hebrews chapter 9, we are told we never have been able to keep the first covenant—that is, to obey the law. The first covenant (the Mosaic Law) had an elaborate system designed to represent the holy presence of God, but by itself this covenant could not bridge the gap between sinful man and holy God.

In verses 11 to 15, the author argues that Jesus, alone, can satisfy fully the demands of God's holiness as an acceptable sacrifice for the sins of His people. All attempts that we make to please God outside of Jesus' sacrifice on the cross are a dead end. These attempts express to God that we think we can obey Him and please Him without Jesus. The author of the book of Hebrews goes on to use an illustration of a legal will in verses 16 to 22. Just as a legal will has no effect until a person dies, so the covenant with God to obtain forgiveness cannot be put into effect without a death—that is, without Jesus' substitutionary death.

Finally, verses 23–28 of Hebrews chapter 9 argue that by the sacrifice of His own life, Jesus was welcomed into the presence of His holy Father (not the earthly Holy of Holies) because He paid the price for the ultimate solution to sin's consequence of eternal separation from God. The argument of the writer of the book of Hebrews is that the conscience of man could not be assuaged by the rituals of the old covenant.

Understanding the Purpose of the Conscience

In the Walt Disney version of the story of Pinocchio, Jiminy Cricket tells Pinocchio, "Let your conscience be your guide." As a general rule, that slogan sounds like good advice. However, the gospel according to Walt Disney is not the gospel according to Jesus Christ. If our conscience can be our infallible guide, why does the Bible say the conscience needs to be cleansed? Both verse 9 and verse 14 indicate that our consciences are not infallible and need to be cleansed.

Definition of Conscience

The conscience as used in the Bible or elsewhere is not a simple term. In fact, in researching I was amazed to discover how complicated the conscience is. If you check out the various definitions from many diverse perspectives, you will see what I mean. You will find religious, secular, and philosophical perspectives of the conscience. For example, evolutionary biology, neuroscience, and sociology, let alone the Bible, all have distinct perceptions of the conscience.

Nevertheless, let's attempt a basic definition of the word *conscience*. The conscience is the processes within our mind that evaluates ourselves in light of certain standards and expectations. These standards are determined by a complex set of values that we are exposed to during our life's journey. When we live according to our values, we have a sense of pleasure. When we violate those values, we suffer mental anguish and feelings of guilt.

The conscience is not entirely a God-given function. As Christians, we tend to believe that the conscience is designed by God to keep us living righteously. Although partially true, in fact some of the functions of the conscience are not only fallible but some aspects of the conscience are actually designed to maintain sinful behaviour rather than alter it.

Romans 2:14–15 (NIV) confirms this point. "Indeed, when Gentiles, who do not have the law, do by nature things required by the law, they are a law for themselves, even though they do not have the law. They show that the requirements of the law are written on their hearts, their consciences also bearing witness, and their thoughts sometimes accusing them and at other times even defending them."

Interestingly, our consciences, which we tend to think work for us, sometimes end up accusing us and, therefore, work for the enemy in condemning us. Or our consciences can excuse us from dealing with the conviction of the Holy Spirit—because the world, our parents, or legalistic Christianity have placed a lesser standard in our conscience. So what good is our conscience—or maybe the real question we need to ask is: is there such a thing as a good conscience?

CHAPTER 17

WHAT IS A GOOD OR
A CLEAR CONSCIENCE?

The most frequent reference in Scripture to the word *conscience* is the phrase or expression "a good or clear conscience." It appears ten times in the Bible. As an example of this phrase, Paul says, "I thank my God, whom I serve, as my ancestors did, with a clear conscience, as night and day I constantly remember you in my prayers." (2 Timothy 1:3)

A good or clear conscience is not necessarily related to faith in Christ, nor to doing absolute good all the time. Conscience is the result of sincere, consistent living in accordance with one's values, whether or not those values are godly or Biblical. Paul did not limit his good conscience to a time after his conversion only—he had honestly been following what he believed was right even before conversion. He persecuted the early Christians because he thought he was doing what was right in order to protect the Old Testament law.

So a good conscience enables us to live consistently according to our inner values, whether or not those values are in themselves good or godly. That is why you cannot appeal to someone to become a Christian on the basis of his conscience. If it is consistent with what he believes, he will see no need to change. As we will see later, a good conscience is no substitute for the work of the Holy Spirit in convicting us, or the blood of Christ in cleansing us.

In my years of working in counselling at Lethbridge College, I had an excellent dean (boss) for several years. He treated me with respect and he believed in me. He promoted me to chairman of the counselling department, he encouraged me to keep growing professionally. He was happily married and, as well as I could tell, raised his two children to be good citizens. One day, he and I were having a meal together. I shared the good news of Jesus with him. He listened attentively and then said to me, "I believe I already live that way. Why do I need Jesus in my life? I live with a clear conscience." In appealing to his conscience to show him he needed Jesus, he dismissed my appeal because, according to him, his conscience basically was clear. I shouldn't have appealed to his conscience.

Faulty Conscience Development

So how does the conscience develop in children and where does it become faulty and therefore unreliable? In Romans 2:15, Paul wrote that our consciences are built on universal, divinely given moral principles that are written on human hearts. But the Bible also says that the conscience can be "seared." It can be dulled into insensitivity by:

1. persistent involvement with sin,
2. abandoning Biblical teachings,

3. dabbling in demonic ideas,
4. childhood training in believing evil is good and good is evil.

As we see, the conscience can be weakened through sin. On the other hand, it can also be strengthened by believing in the truth of God's Word. Our consciences can be trained by the teachings and actions of others, particularly by parents in the early developmental years. In these early years, the child also learns about guilt. Guilt and the conscience play an integral part in the child's early spiritual, mental, and emotional development. When parents are good models of approval and encouragement, the child learns to use guilt in a positive way. But where the home is primarily punitive, critical, and fear-ridden, the child will carry a false sense of guilt in his conscience.

Is the conscience any help to us? Yes, as faulty as it can be at times, if the conscience is properly trained in Biblical understanding it can serve us well by keeping us on track in obeying God and living righteously. In Acts 24, Paul told Felix, the governor, that his desire was to "strive always to keep my conscience clear before God and man" (v. 16 NIV).

The Greek word in the New Testament translated *conscience* is *suneidesis*. The noun form appears thirty times and the verb form (*sundidon/sunoida*) occurs only four times. Paul is the most frequent user of suneidesis (twenty-two times). Hebrews uses the word five times and Peter uses it three times. No Hebrew term in the Old Testament is a linguistic equivalent to the New Testament *suneidesis*, but the use of the word *heart* approximates the concept of self-awareness in certain passages.

Definition of Types of Guilt

I have already written about the difference between true and false guilt and subjective and objective guilt. If you are still not clear on this understanding of guilt, I refer you back to **Appendix 3** to review a Biblical understanding of guilt. This passage of Scripture in Hebrews 9 tells us that we cannot find our way to God through either external religious forms or internal forms of satisfying our own consciences.

Let's reread this last section of Hebrews 9 (NIV) again.

23 It was necessary, then, for the copies of the heavenly things to be purified with these sacrifices, but the heavenly things themselves with better sacrifices than these.

24 For Christ did not enter a man-made sanctuary that was only a copy of the true one; he entered heaven itself, now to appear for us in God's presence.

25 Nor did he enter heaven to offer himself again and again, the way the high priest enters the Most Holy Place every year with blood that is not his own.

26 Then Christ would have had to suffer many times since the creation of the world. But now he has appeared once for all at the end of the ages to do away with sin by the sacrifice of himself.

27 Just as man is destined to die once, and after that to face judgment,

28 so Christ was sacrificed once to take away the sins of many; and he will appear a second time, not to bear sin, but to bring salvation to those who are waiting for him.

The Intercessory Work of Christ

Since the Fall of man at Eden, our consciences have functioned as an internal law, with its own courtroom, its own prosecuting and defense attorneys, its own judge, and its own sentencing system. As long as we remain independent of Christ, we will continuously bring ourselves to trial and pass judgment on ourselves. However, our own efforts at self-administered justice will never quiet our consciences. Jesus' death on the cross alone has paid the penalty for humanity's sin in order to clear the conscience. Nothing man can do ever will satisfy a holy God.

However, even when we are born again we can still fall into the trap of Satan. His trap is to get us to think we can keep God satisfied through external religious forms or internal forms of satisfying our own consciences. How many times have we tried to cleanse our consciences through our own efforts? This attempt has led to acts of death in our spiritual lives. Such is exactly the truth that Hebrews 9:14 expresses. "How much more, then, will the blood of Christ, who through the eternal Spirit offered himself unblemished to God, cleanse our consciences from acts that lead to death, so that we may serve the living God!" (Hebrews 9:14 NIV)

We must see that we have been made perfect in the sight of God by Jesus' sacrifice on the cross. He is like a smiling father looking down at us, as pleased with us as He ever will be. When Satan uses the processes of our consciences to accuse us, we say with Paul in Rom. 8:33 NIV: "Who will bring a charge against God's elect? God is the one who justifies." When we are prone to punish and condemn ourselves for our failures and sins, we must remember **we have no right to do so** because Jesus has already taken care of our sin at the cross. Today,

Christ intercedes for us at the right hand of God on the basis of His completed work on the cross.

Accepting the Forgiveness of Jesus

This self-condemnation also means that we cannot forgive ourselves—a common misunderstanding of many Christians today. I have heard it taught in churches, read it in well-meaning books, heard it proclaimed on television, and personally argued with others about the fallacy of this lie. Nowhere in Scripture are we told to forgive ourselves. If we could, Jesus would have died in vain. Check it out for yourselves by looking up every occurrence of the word "forgiveness" in the Bible. You simply cannot find it in the Scriptures (I will expand more on this misunderstanding later in the book).

The forgiveness of our sins was costly—just ask Jesus (and His Father as well). Forgiveness does not pretend that sin never happened. Rather it acknowledges the pain, the anger, the violation, and then chooses to cancel the debt based on "someone" paying the price for the debt. The person who paid that debt is Jesus Christ. Because of our sin, Father God (who is holy and cannot be in the presence of sin) separated Himself from Jesus for that time He was on the cross. Jesus paid the entire price for our sin. We can never forgive ourselves, we can only **receive** forgiveness from one who has paid the price. Therefore, we are instructed to work **from** our acceptance and forgiveness, not **for** our acceptance and forgiveness.

We must give up our efforts at earning the approval of God through our consciences. We must give up condemning ourselves when we fall short. We can only accept Christ's finished work on the cross as enough. We look to Him alone for the complete and adequate payment for our sins. How will you know you have done this? You know by the freedom you experience when you confess and repent of your sin. You receive His cleansing when you confess your sins, but His forgiveness is already completed at the cross two thousand years ago. We go to God in humility, receiving His cleansing rather than withdrawing from him in pride and trying to forgive ourselves.

Working Out Our Salvation

So how should we respond to guilt in order to keep our conscience clear? First, stop being afraid of guilt by trying to deny or repress it. Let your guilt feelings be the signal that leads you to the cross to see that Jesus has paid the total price for your sin. Then, having thanked God for your forgiveness completed in Christ, confess to God (and to others you trust) what the Holy Spirit has shown you through your guilt. Then repent of believing the lie that has led you to sin in the first place; turn to God's perfect standard of righteousness as your guide. Finally, choose to walk in obedience to what the Holy Spirit has shown you as truth.

Keep Your Eyes on Jesus

We must always keep our eyes focused on Jesus. He alone has the answer to our many questions about living in the joy of Father God's presence and the freedom only He can give. Many of us still have vague, even contradictory, ideas about who God is. This contradiction results in angry, frustrated Christians who constantly carry a heavy burden of guilt and failure for not "measuring up." They withdraw from a loving Father rather than run to embrace Him. A conscience that is not cleansed often creates negative shame in the life of a Christian.

Living with a clear conscience brings much joy in serving God. We delight in telling others about our Christian experience because we now are full of life. As believers today, we need a much greater revelation of the truth about Jesus. We need to experience Jesus Christ's awesome beauty, splendor, love, and mercy, understanding that all of His majesty is because of His completed work at the cross.

We need a fresh revelation of what He has done for us, to understand how completely He has forgiven us. Only then will we find ourselves longing to be in the Father's presence in our daily lives. We need to hear Father God say, "Oh I love you so much. I have such enjoyment in you—you fill me with great pleasure. You are my son or my daughter and I delight in you."

Now let's discuss how shame gets developed in us through our childhood experiences.

PART 4

THE DEVELOPMENT OF
SHAME IN CHILDHOOD

CHAPTER 18

A Bit of My
Childhood Story

Years ago I was teaching a workshop in Ontario. My good friend, David Campbell, a longtime pastor in Owen Sound, was driving me from Owen Sound to another town a number of miles away to meet with some other pastors. As we drove, we passed several small towns along the way. In rural Ontario, every little town has a graveyard on the outskirts. As we drove, my mind wandered to this thought: *I wonder what kind of stories lie under the grave markers of all those people buried in those cemeteries.*

Childhood experiences are, for many people, a graveyard of markers. Those markers indicate "death experiences," pain that has left indelible imprints on their hearts. If we were able to go back in time and remember, we would see "places" where numerous hurts and pains were buried. Because we were children at that time, the only way we could respond to the pain was bury it, thinking maybe the hurt would go away over time.

Many people believe that time heals pain—but that thinking is false. Time will push pain out of our conscious awareness but the pain is still there, waiting to surface in another form at an inopportune time. Some experiences in childhood were minor. Some were major and extremely hurtful. However, even minor experiences accumulated over many years make a big impact on our psyches.

Some of my Personal Childhood Experiences

I want to be vulnerable with you and share some of my own graveyard markers. I hope you will see, through the journey of some of my childhood experiences, the impact in my adult years. As I mentioned before, I grew up in a family of six children. My parents married in 1945 after World War II. My father had been wounded seriously in battle in Sicily and was in rehab in England for two years, from 1943 to 1945. When he returned to Canada, he married my mother, whom he had known as a friend for eighteen years.

The Bretherick household was a busy place. Because my parents had two sets of twins (I was one twin), they had six children in six years. In addition to the eight of us living in one home, my maternal grandparents also lived in a suite in the basement of our large house. If I recall correctly—it was, after all a long time ago—as children we were quite competitive with each other. I struggled with a great deal of insecurity as a child. I also wrestled with inferiority because I was a twin.

Of course I now know inferiority is a lie, because each person is created unique in God's plan (even identical twins, which my brother Grant and I are not). Throughout my childhood I developed a strategy to survive in our busy household. Because of my own insecurities in this competitive family, I needed to win when we played games. If it didn't look like I could win, I would try to find a way to withdraw without losing face. If my siblings read this book, I'm sure they will likely say, "Yeah, we knew that about Graham."

In my thinking, if I lost at a game, it was not just a "game." For me, losing at anything was a life issue. It confirmed to me that I was a "loser." The "loss" confirmed my deep suspicions that I was an inferior being. If I could sense I was going to lose, I would say, "I don't feel like playing anymore." Sometimes I could sense I was going to lose even before we started the game; then I made a decision not to play. If I knew one of my siblings was much better at a certain game I made an excuse, saying I wasn't interested in that game.

Sports Day

At times when I couldn't get out of the "game," I had to participate. That was especially so in elementary school on sports day. Once a year in the month of June, the school would have a competitive sports day of various races and relays. (This was in the "good ole' days" when competition was actually encouraged in school.)

In the elementary school we attended, the teachers divided the participants of our grade into two groups, depending on when their birthdays occurred in the calendar year. Because my brother Grant and I were born in December, we were placed in the younger category. Only three of us were in this age category—Grant, me, and another student named Larry. I had no choice but to take part in sports day because my mother, who was a nurse, saw through my attempts at faking sickness. In the races between the three of us, Larry and Grant were fairly competitive but I was always third (which was really last!). If you got first place, you received a blue ribbon. For second, the ribbon was red. If you were third, the colour of the ribbon was white (like a quiet surrender).

At the end of sports day, Grant and Larry shared blue and red ribbons and Graham had a chest full of white ribbons. If you didn't know only three of us were in the race it might not look so bad, but most of the other students watched us race—and my chest full of white ribbons spelled "loser." I experienced the "shame" of losing at every sports day. I remember having tears at the end of what was supposed to be a fun day. For a boy, tears spelled disaster because in addition to being a loser, I was a crybaby. In the shame of my tears, sometimes anger would spill over because I was hurting inside.

You may be thinking, *It happened in early childhood a long time ago, so what is the big deal?* But I buried a lot of those feelings of shame from childhood; they didn't surface until the vulnerable years of adolescence. I found I functioned the same way in my teenage years and even carried some of it over into my adult years. If I was able to win, I made sure I won in a big way so I could gloat over my win. I felt good when I won, yet carried a false sense of security because I would surely lose again.

My Academic Development

Going through junior and senior high school became a major challenge for me academically. I had so little confidence in myself; I didn't study or try hard. I didn't even graduate at the end of grade 12, because I failed my final year of math. I worked for a year prior to attending

Bible College. Even then, I almost failed the first year in Bible college because I wasn't disciplined in my time and my work habits.

I remember, toward the end of my first year, being aware that I was not going to pass if I didn't "pull up my socks." How do you flunk out of Bible College? Yikes! I pushed very hard to get all my delinquent essays and assignments completed. I motivated myself to study—to avoid the shame of failing my courses. I would stay up until 4:30 in the morning, get two hours of sleep, and then stumble to class because the college rules prohibited missing class.

After the struggles of that year, in the summer months I vowed I wouldn't let myself fall behind again. I discovered I actually had a brain hidden in all that grey matter. In the second year of Bible College I disciplined my time, made a good effort, and my marks improved dramatically. That's when I realized that I could become important through academic studies. I convinced myself that when I became well educated, people would consider me successful.

Church Split

My pursuit of education was done with mixed motives. I found myself critical of others whom I surmised were not "smart" like me (actually, I really wasn't all that smart). Several years later, in my mid thirties, God allowed me to crash. The church I coplanted with a good friend fell apart through a split. Some of these friends turned on me and left the church. I was so disillusioned that I denied my faith (like Peter) and wanted nothing more to do with God. Sherry could not believe the words that were coming from my mouth. I was badly hurt and disillusioned with God, the church, and Christianity.

Fortunately this denial only lasted two days, because God sent two Christian brothers, John and Terry, to tell me the impossibility of running from God. Nevertheless I was a broken man, full of anger. However, I did work through my repentance; God used this time to awaken me to all the unresolved issues in my life. I dared to open the "closet of shame" a little and let in some light to expose hidden areas of my life.

At that time, I invited Duane Harder to help me deal with this deep insecurity. Within a year, I asked him to be my personal pastor and spiritual father. He gently (and sometimes not so gently) probed away at the hidden issues in my life that caused my shame. Much of this pain was so buried in my childhood that I didn't realize its extent. Some of those experiences were so shameful that I made vows (unconscious to me) never to "open the door for anyone to look inside."

Interestingly, every time I taught my workshop on shame, inevitably people came asking to share their hearts with me. They want to tell me something that they have never told anyone. Because I had been open and vulnerable in the workshop, they took the risk of trusting me to share their painful experiences. After listening to me, they knew they needed to open their own "shame closets." I am always glad to hear people's confessions and to bring them before God to receive His cleansing and freedom.

Vows Are Powerful

The vows we make to protect ourselves are very powerful. In those vows, we have told ourselves we will never let anyone know about this sin, failure, or shameful experience of the past. Let me say to you: if you are not yet able to "open the door," do not heap more shame on yourself. Ask God to give you the courage to share with the right person at the right time. Daring to open the "closed door of shame" helps break the power of shame in our lives. When we can talk about our shame in a safe environment, we gain significant power over it.

As you are reading this book, I don't want to use undue pressure to manipulate you to open your hearts before you are ready. I have been on a journey for a long time, or I could not share as openly with you as I have. I want to bring you hope, not condemnation. God has a right time for our exposure; He does give us an invitation to open our hearts to Him. Revelation 3:20: "Here I am! I stand at the door and knock. If anyone hears my voice and opens the door, I will come in and eat with that person, and they with me." The Holy Spirit waits for you to open the door.

CHAPTER 19

THE USE OF SHAME
IN PARENTING

Shame is like a wound in the self. Frequently, this shame is instilled at a young age. It can be the result of rebukes given harshly, warnings given without sensitivity, teasing, ridicule, ostracism, any form of rejection from parents, peers, playmates, teachers, or others. Tender, sensitive children take these contemptible voices from outside themselves and begin to internalize them. Most young children do not have adequate self-esteem defences. These outside voices soon become internal voices of shame and disapproval. As children internalize these voices, the lies become part of their identity.

Some of this shame damage is caused by the parenting process, even though most parents dearly love their children. The shaming parental voices result from the insecurity in which many parents operate. Moreover, parents often don't understand the impact of their parenting. Parents frequently feel out of control with the disciplining process. Most parents desire to bring about conformity of obedience in their children. However, knowingly or unknowingly they use shame to control their children's behaviour. At times, shame is used unknowingly because parents are simply parenting the way they were parented.

Using Shame to Control

However, at times parents are so desperate to deal with their children's disobedience they knowingly use shame for control. They use statements like, "That's disgusting" and, "You should be ashamed of yourself." When we tie those two statements together, we have attempted to correct his behaviour by shaming the child. The child's behaviour may be wrong, but to call their behaviour disgusting and adding the word "shame" creates another level of difficulty for the child.

When I was around age seven or eight, I had some bowel control problems. I was an insecure, anxious, uptight child with a great deal of control issues in my life. It was all part of trying to fight the insecurity I felt. As a result, I had problems with constipation (I just love talking about this—NOT!). I would refrain from having a bowel movement because of the pain and then by the time I really had to go, it was an even more painful experience. This process occurred repeatedly.

In the meantime, my underwear was often soiled. My dear mother was getting exasperated with always having to scrub my dirty underwear. One day, out of frustration, she said to me as she held up my underwear, "I'm not scrubbing your underwear anymore. You will do it yourself from now on." I know she didn't mean to, but she definitely did shame me. Especially so because two of my siblings were in the same room and overheard.

I can remember taking my underwear, going to the bathroom,

locking the door, and with tears in my eyes scrubbing them. I was experiencing intensive shame, yet didn't know how to deal with constipation. Nor did I know how to deal with the shame I was feeling. I recognize now that my mother had her hands full with six children, plus her two parents living with us who were both needy. She had a busy household to maintain. My mother was an excellent mother overall but we all have made those mistakes in our parenting and have lived to regret them. As an aside, I have since forgiven my mother for shaming me.

The irony of this whole situation was at the time we attended a Baptist church, and the denomination was called Regular Baptists. I was, however, anything but regular. I can laugh now but I was definitely not laughing during those days. (Today the denomination is called the Fellowship of Evangelical Baptists). Eventually, I overcame this physical problem but the experience was painful emotionally.

The shame of those memories stuck with me for a long time. Yet the larger issue was that I internalized this shame; I felt a great deal of shame about myself throughout my growing years. To compensate for this sense of shame, I added controls to my life to keep the shame at bay. I was trying to control the shame by controlling my behaviour, even though at the time I had no idea shame actually controlled me.

Not Working Through Childhood Shame

Our unresolved shame issues from childhood often repeat themselves into adulthood. When we don't work through those childhood shame experiences, we also are prevented from accepting our own children in their areas of weakness. To the degree that we have not dealt with our shame issues, we will pass those issues on to our children (whether or not we are aware of it). Even if we are conscious of not wanting to pass on these issues to our children we likely will pass them anyway, because shame still functions in us as adults.

That is why I appeal to parents (and even adults who are not parents) to deal with their unresolved fears, guilt, bitterness, or shame issues. Moreover, I am motivated to deal with my "stuff" because, to the best of my ability, I do not want to pass these unresolved issues on to my children. I can't avoid passing my sin nature on to my children; that is inevitable. But I don't want to pass on to them any more negativity than is necessary given my fallen sin nature.

Shame Is Contagious

Shame is contagious. When a child grows up with adults who are living in shame, these adults feel powerless in their world; the child will pick up shame from his parents. Obviously this shame is not often verbalized but nevertheless appears in behaviour, attitudes, and nonverbal messages. I wonder if my father was ashamed of his anger outbursts but didn't know how to deal with the anger stored within him. I think he thought of himself as patient (considering he was raising six children, his patience was exceptional) but when his "patience" ran out, he would "lose it."

As I looked back to my thirties, I remember feeling ashamed of the way I used anger when I disciplined my children. I loved my father dearly—he was a good man—but when he got angry we took "cover." Because I hid my anger toward my father by not dealing with it, I grew up feeling ashamed of my own anger reactions. As a result, I acted the same way as he did when I started parenting my children.

When Sam, our oldest son, was about ten years old, I lost control one day. I did what my father did to me. I vowed I would never treat my children the way my father treated me when unable to contain his anger—but I was doing what I vowed I would never do. When I was about sixteen years old, I remember vowing never to treat my children the way my father treated me when he was angry.

Anger in the Shame Closet

Part of the reason I couldn't control my anger was because I had a lot of unresolved bitterness locked up in my "shame closet." At that time, I didn't know how to deal with my buried anger. To make things more difficult, my father died about seven years earlier. Because I loved my father, I did not want to dishonour him. (I still desire to honour my father to this day.) But like all fathers, my dad made mistakes caused by what he didn't deal with in his life.

In desperation that day, I asked the Lord what was wrong with me. He gently opened the closet and brought me to face my hidden shame. We have to deal with the buried anger hidden behind the "shame door" before we can deal effectively with our present anger issues.

I remember, years ago, counselling with a young woman whose mother was extremely overprotective. Her mother had a great deal of wounding from her birth family, including many shame issues. She told me a story about her mother being on a school bus as a child. She was being teased mercilessly and ran off the bus in tears at her stop. She realized that her mother wrestled with feelings of insecurity, which manifested in shy behaviour. She didn't know how to deal with all her fears and hurts. I suspect her mother made numerous vows never to allow her children to go through what she went through in childhood.

Due to her vows, she overprotected her four children. All of them struggled with significant insecurity as they grew up. In trying to protect them, she didn't prepare them for life. Because this mother was not able (or willing) to deal with her own shame issues, she passed her shame to her children, the opposite of what she wanted to do.

Internalizing Judgments

When a child internalizes negative judgments about himself, a part of him cringes in shame. This sets off a series of defense mechanisms and compensatory behaviours that can eventually become part of his personality. When a child who lives in shame is corrected by his parents, instead of receiving the correction as something helpful, he immediately judges himself as inadequate.

When the child is disciplined in an incorrect manner, he further sees himself as an inadequate person. For example, in correcting a child, you tell him or her, "You are a bad boy or bad girl." You have just shamed your child. This is quite unlike telling your child, "Johnny, hitting your brother is wrong. I know you are angry at him for taking the toy you were playing with, but hitting him to get your toy back is wrong." When expressed this way, even with intensity, you are not shaming the child but correcting him, giving him a better way to deal with his behaviour.

Psalm 127:3 (NIV): "Sons are a heritage from the Lord, children a reward from him. Like arrows in the hands of a warrior are sons born in one's youth. Blessed is the man whose quiver is full of them. They will not be put to shame when they contend with their enemies in the gate."

This verse reminds us that when we raise children God's way, they will not have to contend with unresolved shame later in life when they are dealing with their enemies. The best defense against shame is to love children consistently. This doesn't mean perfectly, because perfection is impossible. Consistently means that we, as parents, are free to own our mistakes by asking our children to forgive us when we err in our parenting.

Parenting without Shame

When we parent without shame, we can take ownership for our mistakes by acknowledging wrong and asking our children for their forgiveness. Without question, I have made many mistakes in my parenting. But I have learned to do what I am advising you; as a result, I earned my children's respect. All my children said to me in cards or verbal expression something like, "Dad, we know you made lots of mistakes, but what we appreciate about you is your willingness to own your mistakes and be real with us."

Many parents feel that if they take ownership for their weaknesses, their children will disrespect them. However, the opposite is true. When children see reality in their parents, they respond to that reality by respecting them. We often think we should train our children by hiding our flaws from them—but they are far more perceptive than we think. In our love for our children, we want to be sensitive enough to appreciate the uniqueness of each child. That way, our children can accept themselves in their strengths and weaknesses without living in shame.

The child living in a shame-free environment learns to accept himself. He doesn't feel he has to compete with his siblings or other children for a place of acceptance. Every child asks the question of himself, "Am I important enough to you to be special?" If you have multiple children, they all want and need to be special in their parents' eyes.

CHAPTER 20

THE EFFECTS OF ACCUMULATED EXPERIENCES OF SHAME

From infancy through adolescence, children are living through shame experiences. As these shame experiences accumulate, they have a significant effect on a child's development. The effect of shame in a child's life begins in the first year of life. Let me give an example. When an infant seeks to engage a parent's attention with "coos," eye contact, and attention-seeking behaviours, if mother is unwilling or unable to give attention at that moment, the child experiences rejection.

If, at that point, the child internalizes rejection, he will experience shame. Infants are not able to function cognitively like adults. They communicate through their emotions. Sometimes, mother is caught in her busyness and forgets to respond to her child's reaching out for acceptance. That is why eye contact and touch are extremely important for communicating acceptance to a child. The shame of that moment can be reversed quickly if in the next moment the mother responds with acceptance.

If, however, mother (or father) consistently fails to meet the child's need for affirmation through emotional contact, then that will be the start of shame in infancy. Whenever we experience rejection and the rejection is not reversed, the accumulated effect results in shame. This process remains true from childhood to adolescence to adulthood.

John Paul Jackson's Story

I read a story years ago about the late John Paul Jackson. He shared this story to illustrate the impact of rejection in the development of shame. John had a powerful prophetic gift that touched many people's lives. (Our daughter Sarah and her husband Graham told us they had been given a prophetic word by John at a conference in England some years ago.) The story John tells about himself is quite humorous, but also poignant about the effects of rejection in his early life.

When I was twelve years old, I was smitten with Charlotte. I would ride my bike three-and-a-half miles to the ballpark simply to catch a glimpse of her. With each possible encounter, my heart seemed as if it would leap from my chest at the mere thought that she might be there. Day and night she filled my thoughts. With all the intensity, purity, and innocence I could muster, I "loved" Charlotte. I was desperate to see her as often as possible.

One fateful day, I even begged God, "Please make Charlotte come to this ball game. Please."

A crowd filled the stands behind the backstop, but there was no sign of Charlotte. With each passing inning, my heart sank deeper. In despair, I slumped down onto a weathered gray bleacher and began to sulk. But just when I thought all hope was lost, I heard the sound of her voice. As I looked up, I saw the radiance of her hair as the light gently wove its way through each strand. Two other girls were standing with her, but I didn't even notice. For a moment the world was in balance, and no one, not even her snooty friends, could stop my feelings for Charlotte.

As I sat mesmerized, I began to face my fears. I had never let any girl know that I liked her, let alone one as perfect and beautiful as Charlotte. But that day, things were going to change! With the coolest walk and with all the courage I could muster, I moved toward her.

At ninety-eight pounds, with my legs shaking, my lungs like iron, my heart pounding, and sweat dripping off my skin, I started sauntering toward her. But an obstacle stood between us that I had not anticipated: a water pipe sticking up just above the dirt. The spring rain had weathered the dirt away, leaving the pipe exposed. Naturally, my huge foot would find it and trip over it. Suddenly, as if in slow motion, I was falling. My gangly arms flailed as I tried in vain to get my hands out of my jeans pockets and in front of me.

It was too late. My face hit the ground at full speed. My shoe was still stuck under the water pipe. Hours seemed to go by. Inside, I cried out to God and asked why He had let this happen to me. I was humiliated. I scrambled and crawled to hide behind the bleachers. Peeking through the slats, I was pleasantly shocked: Charlotte hadn't seen me, and she was still busy talking to her friends. There is a God, I thought. All is well! But I would soon find out why my devastation hadn't been noticed by her sky-blue eyes.

My face and clothes were filthy from the inch-thick dust I had fallen into. Spitting dirt from my mouth, I made my way over to the next ball field, where there was a water fountain. There I could be hidden from Charlotte's critical eye while I washed myself.

I soon realized I couldn't get all the dirt out of my white T-shirt, so I turned it inside out, hoping Charlotte wouldn't notice. And so, with a pounding heart and great uncertainty, I made my way toward Charlotte, finally reaching her and leaning heavily against a nearby chain-link fence.

Trying to sound manly, yet with an awkward, cracking voice, I said, "Hi. Are you here to watch your brother play?"

Charlotte gracefully spun around and looked at me. I could hardly wait to hear her words. "John, I think you are really cute," she said.

My heart leaped like a rocket aimed for the moon. The girl I adored felt the same way about me! I was in heaven, it seemed. I didn't even get a chance to say my well-rehearsed pickup line. She beat me to my amorous proclamation. It was then that I heard the rest of the story.

"But I already have a dog." Charlotte giggled at her awful comment and twirled around while her friends laughed at me. Just as quickly as I was sent soaring by her first seven words, I was completely crushed by her final six. With tears rising in my eyes, I silently found my bike and walked home. I would have ridden the bike, but I was crying so hard that I couldn't see. I took the back roads home so no one would see me crying. Caught in rejection's matrix, I kept thinking, She thinks I'm a dog. I felt lost and alone, hopeless and mortified.

The summer passed and Charlotte moved away. I didn't think of her again for twenty-five years. When I did, I began the arduous journey toward healing. (I have asked for permission to use this story from John Paul Jackson and they granted me that in an email)

Perhaps you can relate to his story and have had similar experiences of rejection in your life. Chances are that most of us could tell our own stories of rejection that are just as poignant. I certainly could.

If a child or a teenager experiences too many instances of shame, he will not be receptive to his parents' correction in discipline. When a parent tries to correct a child's behaviour, internalized shame in the child blocks his ability to separate himself as a "bad" person from his behavioural mistakes.

If the child experiences too many instances of shame, the shame will inhibit the child's ability to separate between himself as "bad" and his behaviour as "bad" when a parent tries to correct the child's behaviour. The child will associate his wrong behaviour with feelings of shame. He will associate what he has done (behaviour) with feelings of shame. Those shame feelings teach him that he is unacceptable when he behaves in a wrong way.

Shame Blocks the Door to the Guilt Signal

The pain of rejection is often stuffed behind the "closed door of shame," only to surface again when more correction is needed in the child's life. Shame now blocks the door to guilt, which is the emotional signal that God has given us to correct our behaviour and get us back onto the path of right behaviour. The guilt signal has been given to the child to show where he can correct his own mistakes. Shame inhibits the child from a correct use of the guilt signal.

Before a young child has learned how to use his God-given guilt signal, his parents are the guilt signal for the child. The infant child has not yet learned the difference between right and wrong. In the training process, the parents affirm what is right and correct what is wrong. Slowly, the child begins to internalize right from wrong. In time, the child will become aware of when he has sinned and done something wrong.

By the time children are in their teens, they will know right from wrong in the area of morality if they have been raised with moral standards. Even though they often choose wrong because of the rebellion and sin nature in them, they nevertheless know the difference. If you are raising teenagers, you will see an ongoing journey for them to make the right choices for godly behaviour.

If the child can't respond to parents' correction because the guilt signals are confused, then the child is in a precarious place. To enter adulthood facing all the decisions before them without clarity of ethical and moral behaviour is dangerous. This situation is magnified with foster children in the home. The foster parent may not have experienced the opportunity to build a sense of right and wrong from the beginning. Trying to bring correction to a foster child is often more difficult than raising birth children.

Children Are Always Acceptable

Children will often associate wrong behaviour with "I'm a bad person." Therefore, they reject the correction, because it is too difficult to accept that rejection on an ongoing basis. Of great importance is to communicate to a child that even though he makes a mistake or chooses a rebellious behaviour, he is always acceptable. Mistakes can be forgiven, corrected, or reversed. Children need to know that they always will be loved by their parents no matter how badly they behave. Parents still need to discipline, correct, and punish where necessary, but the bottom line is that their children will always feel loved.

God has designed that parents initially act as the guilt signal for their children, until the children are old enough to internalize the various guilt responses and react on their own. This gradual shift throughout childhood slowly causes the child to emerge into an adult who knows the difference between right and wrong, hopefully making right choices. The child's sense of having healthy self-esteem comes from the parents' ability to empathically tune into the child's world. The parents will need to reassure the child repeatedly that he is acceptable no matter how many mistakes are made growing up.

Children will then learn that they can correct their mistakes; they don't have to hide in shame. But when they make a mistake and are shamed for it, what can they do with the shame? The rejection is too painful to deal with, so they place the rejection in the "shame closet" to put it out of their conscious minds. Children who are not taught to correct their mistakes are covered in shame. They will feel like a failure and identify as a failure, which makes it hard for them to prepare for success in adulthood.

A Shameful Self-Concept

As a result, children will develop a shameful self-concept and continually will maintain low self-esteem and rejection. There are three common coping mechanisms for dealing with unresolved shame: defiance, compliance, or withdrawal. In defiance, children will use anger or rebellion as a means of self-protection. In compliance, they will attempt to please everyone by being a "nice" person. If they choose withdrawal, they will do what they can to protect themselves by staying away from interaction with people. These are three common responses for dealing with shame.

The parents' role is to observe shame-based behaviours. When we see such behaviours in our children, we need to find a natural way to validate them. We correct where necessary, but also help them overcome the tendency to confuse making mistakes with being a "bad" person. If a child has made a mistake or misbehaved, calling himself names like "stupid or idiot," then you know he is shaming himself as a means of correcting behaviour.

The child who shames himself with derogatory names will begin to believe that he is too "stupid" to correct his behaviour. The parent needs to challenge the child's perception that he is "stupid" and tell him not to believe that about himself. We can affirm that he made a mistake but we can also help him correct his behaviour, showing him how to do it rightly. When a child shames himself, he thinks he has corrected the problem by putting himself down. He merely has punished himself with a shaming statement, but no correction of behaviour has taken place.

The Use of the "Rod"

When parents don't deal with the emotional shaming process in their children, the children will continue to internalize this sense of shame. In time, shame becomes a part of their self-concept; they identify themselves in this way. Because our North American culture has moved away from using corporal punishment (spanking), we correct our children with shame instead. I often observe younger parents using withdrawal of love as a corrective punishment. Shamed-based correction is not an effective way to change behaviour.

Despite the heavy influence of humanism in our modern parenting styles, the Bible teaches that the "rod" is God's method of dealing with the spirit of rebellion in a child. The "rod" in Scripture represents authority. God, who is the ultimate authority, has given parents His authority over their children; He expects them to use authority correctly. There is clearly no place in the Bible for beating a child with uncontrolled anger. Such is an abuse of the authority that God has given parents.

Parents who were abused as children often vow never to spank their children because of what they have been through. As a result, their children become a behaviour problem. Without the proper use of correction, children grow more unruly year by year. Unfortunately, parents then resort to shaming to try to correct their children's behaviour.

Proverbs 13:18 (NIV) reminds us that "He who ignores discipline comes to poverty and shame but whoever heeds correction is honoured." If parents want their children to grow up to "honour" (that is, like) themselves, they need proper correction as children. Shame-based children will not like themselves and therefore not like (honour) their parents as they get older. When we reject what God has said in His Word about parenting our children, the result will be a society in rebellion and chaos, as we are seeing a great deal today.

When I was in university, my Bible-based thinking was highly criticized. When I wrote term papers on parenting, they were often challenged by my humanistic professors. I tried hard to stay true to what I believed the Bible taught, but I can now see that I was influenced more than I realized by my university training. For example, I chose to spank my children with my hand rather than the rod. I did this because I "reasoned" (through humanistic thinking) that I would have a better sense of how much I was hurting my children when I spanked them. However, when I reached out to comfort my children after I had spanked them they drew back from me, because my hand was now a weapon. It was only after my spiritual father, Duane Harder, challenged me to do a Biblical study of the word "rod" that I realized I needed to repent for my disobedience toward God's Word.

God Uses Punishment for Our Development

God is not reluctant to use punishment when needed. His first desire is always to love His children. But the Bible also says that God punishes those He loves. Hebrews 12:4–13 (NIV) tells us:

4   In your struggle against sin, you have not yet resisted to the point of shedding your blood.

5   And have you completely forgotten this word of encouragement that addresses you as a father addresses his son? It says,
"My son, do not make light of the Lord's discipline,
and do not lose heart when he rebukes you,

6   because the Lord disciplines the one he loves,
and he chastens everyone he accepts as his son."

7   Endure hardship as discipline; God is treating you as his children. For what children are not disciplined by their father?

8   If you are not disciplined—and everyone undergoes

discipline—then you are not legitimate, not true sons and daughters at all.

9   Moreover, we have all had human fathers who disciplined us and we respected them for it. How much more should we submit to the Father of spirits and live!

10 They disciplined us for a little while as they thought best; but God disciplines us for our good, in order that we may share in his holiness.

11 No discipline seems pleasant at the time, but painful. Later on, however, it produces a harvest of righteousness and peace for those who have been trained by it.

12 Therefore, strengthen your feeble arms and weak knees.

13 "Make level paths for your feet," so that the lame may not be disabled, but rather healed.

Most of us don't like using corrective punishment because we either have had it used wrongly on ourselves, or we have been influenced by humanistic psychology. I realize what I am sharing here is not popular at all today, but I believe it needs to be addressed. The shame-based discipline that I see today is doing far more damage than the overuse of the rod ever has done (in saying this, I am NOT justifying the wrong use of corporal punishment at all).

Many people have carried unresolved shame issues from childhood into their discipline processes with their children. Because of a lack of any real solution to correcting children's behaviour, the cycle continues generation after generation. The shame behaviours of children result in unresolved shame issues in adulthood—we wonder why we struggle with shame in adult living.

I once counselled a man who was struggling with low self-esteem and identity issues. He said that he did not feel free. He felt "all locked up." I asked him if he knew the cause. He told me that when he cried as a young boy, his father shamed him. Eventually, he came to the conclusion that crying was unmanly. As an adult male he could not express tears and he was unable to express any emotions, except anger. He wouldn't allow himself to cry because he felt so shamed.

To work through these problems, we had to break a number of lies that he believed. He also had to work through anger toward his father for the damage done. I believe his father meant well trying to make a man out of a boy, but he was doing it the wrong way.

Braveheart's Impact on Me

I remember vividly the first time I watched the movie, "Braveheart." My son Sam had seen it three times and he urged me to see it. Finally he told me he was taking me to the movie, so I agreed to go. As I watched the movie, I was captivated. (Yes, I know it probably is not historically accurate, but it is still a powerful movie.) I saw the portrayal of Christ throughout the movie. I keenly was aware of the messages of sacrifice and betrayal.

After the movie Sam asked me to go for coffee, but I was overwhelmed by the movie so I turned him down. I knew something large was going off inside of me. As I drove past the main cemetery in Lethbridge, I felt compelled to turn in. I parked by two flaming torches burning there. I started to weep uncontrollably. For the first time in my life, I thought I was totally losing it. I asked the Holy Spirit what was wrong with me. I must have been there half an hour.

Finally I was able to get myself together enough to drive home.

Again, I asked the Holy Spirit to help me understand why I reacted so strongly to the movie. I realized I was ashamed to show my emotions in the theatre. But a greater issue was brought to my attention. I have wondered all my life if I would be willing to suffer and die for Jesus Christ as many saints have done in the past and present.

When I saw William Wallace being tortured on that horizontal cross, I was overwhelmed. The question on my mind was: *Could I be that brave?* Wallace's last cry of "FREEDOM" before he died fully captured the core of the cry of my heart. When that call for freedom went out, I almost burst into tears in the theatre. I deeply identified with William Wallace's refusal to take the easy way out by swallowing the pill that would have made his death much easier.

He made a choice for freedom for his countrymen and the Scotland he loved. He chose suffering for what he believed rather than relief from his pain. I asked myself the question, "Would I have the courage to suffer for what I truly believe rather than choose to protect my life and deny my faith?"

A few days after I saw *Braveheart*, I shared my reaction to the movie with my friend, Craig Webber, who was at the movie that same night. He said to me that he wondered if my emotional response also had to do with the call for freedom on my life. He said, "You have been called by God to set people free." That is true. Bringing others into freedom is the essence of the call God put on my life.

I also realized that I was dealing with shame that tried to hold me back. But God was using that "shameful" experience to touch something deep in my heart, thereby further releasing me into my calling. I wonder how many times our childhood experiences have prevented us from touching the deep emotional wounds in our lives. Some of these wounds are almost indefinable, because we have buried them so deep for so long.

However, our willingness to explore these dark memories may be beneficial in helping us see more clearly why He created us. Daring to overcome the deep, dark secrets of shame is part of our destiny of discovery. Shame experiences that never surface and get worked through may prevent us from knowing the fullness of our calling. Our fear keeps us from exploring the shame limits that God has put in us for His development. Only by the grace of Almighty God dare we go "where no man has ever gone before."

CHAPTER 21

CARRYING CHILDHOOD SHAME
INTO ADULTHOOD

Unhealed emotional shame from childhood has major ramifications for our personalities in adulthood. Here are some examples of what I mean. A great deal of shame and hurt in childhood can distort our expectations of other people. For example, we may tend to see everybody in authority as demanding. When we have a minor conflict with our boss at work, we see him as demanding. Because other colleagues don't see the boss this way, we wonder why.

Unresolved shame from childhood can affect our self-esteem. Shame can cause us to become angry at ourselves, because deep within we don't like who we are. Why? Because we are ashamed of ourselves. Shame can lead to a criticalness of our own behaviours or attitudes; it can spread to being critical of others. Self-criticism (anger at yourself) also can lead to depression, which in turn can lead to suicidal thoughts and maybe suicidal behaviours.

Unresolved Shame's Impact on Us

Unresolved shame can lead to habit patterns in our personalities that are difficult to change. People can become obsessive compulsive (OCD) by not dealing adequately with shame, guilt, and fear. If OCD is not resolved, it can develop into addictive behaviours. We think these addictive behaviours are trying to help us get free from OCD, but addictions only make life worse.

Shame-based behaviours can lead to the early stages of schizophrenia (called borderline schizophrenia). Schizophrenia typically occurs in adolescence when a young person cannot handle the stresses of life. He reverts to a place of protection in his mind called unreality. The mind and the emotions are not working together to solve the pressures of life.

Here is an example: if I told you that your mother just died yet you broke into laughter, I would deduce that you are not handling the reality of that news adequately. The normal human reaction to such bad news is tears and crying. (Of course, if you hated your mother and she was filthy rich, leaving you to inherit millions, the laughter would make sense.) Our emotions are meant to signal us so we can sort out what is going on inside us.

When childhood has many unresolvable problems, the child has to find a way to survive. One way is to repress the emotional signals, eventually shifting one's thinking into a realm of unreality to cope with the immense emotional pain. The more often a person shifts into unreality, the more likely borderline schizophrenia will develop. Over the years of adolescence and later into young adulthood, the condition can worsen and more harmful forms of schizophrenia like paranoid, catatonic, and disorganized schizophrenia can take root.

As this state continues, the chemistry in one's body changes. This change in body chemistry feeds these schizophrenic behaviours. This is why most schizophrenia is treated with psychotropic drugs, an attempt to control the self-destructive behaviours of schizophrenia. In my view, the chemical imbalance does not cause the schizophrenia. Schizophrenia is the result of the unsolvable stress in the adolescent's life.

When the symptoms are treated with drugs the behaviours will appear to be under control, but the person becomes a prisoner of the chemicals that control his life. The root of the problem has not been addressed and the behaviour gradually worsens. The root of much of this type of behaviour is unresolved anger, fear, shame, and guilt, repressed over many years.

Unhealed Shame Experiences

Unhealed shameful experiences in childhood can lead adults into a variety of ineffective behaviours in adulthood. For example, anxiety disorders, general fearfulness, responsiveness to false guilt, paranoid responses to other people and out of control rage can develop. Because many of these childhood traumas are not resolved to a place of healing, they are stored in the "shame closet," only to surface later in life.

A young man came to me for counselling because when he had suffered a major failure in his life, he fell into serious depression. His first comments to me when he came into my office were, "I never imagined myself ever coming to see a 'shrink.'" I said, "Thanks!" I asked him to relate his story so I could understand why he was in this emotional state.

As he shared his history with me, we worked through his adolescent years. I asked him what major issues occurred during that time period. Without thinking, he told me that at fourteen years old, his sister's boyfriend (who was eighteen at the time) sexually molested him. As soon as he spoke, he put his hand over his mouth and said, "I should never have told you. I've never shared that incident with anyone; even my wife doesn't know."

It was clear that he never intended to share this assault with me but since he had, I "stuck my foot in the door," asking whether he wanted to talk about it. I said the "ugly truth" is out now so maybe we should work it through. As he explained more details of that event, it was obvious that he felt guilty as well as ashamed. All these years he thought that HE had invited this sexual behaviour.

I assured him that he was the victim. He definitely had not invited this abuse. I could tell this by examining his nonverbal behaviour—he carried this unwanted sexual experience as if he were the guilty party. Because he had never worked through the issues properly, he was living with false guilt. He had repressed these experiences and they ended up in the "shame closet." Then he "locked the door" to prevent anyone else knowing about it and assumed that he had brought it on himself.

He believed a lie that he had somehow invited this unwanted attention from this eighteen-year-old boyfriend of his sister. I explained the difference between true and false guilt, which helped him work through the legitimate anger and forgiveness needed to set him free. I explained how unresolved false guilt turns into shame and why it was so important to deal with these shame issues from the past. I counselled him over a period of six months.

About a year after I had first met this young man, he phoned me to invite me for lunch. At lunch, he referenced the shame issue and thanked me for persevering in dealing with that incident. He said, "I can't believe the freedom I am now experiencing as a result of working it through." He also talked about how much more freedom he had with regard to his sexual intimacy with his wife. I was delighted to hear that report.

Shame and Addictions

In my experience, those unresolved shame incidents are common. Essentially, we have believed that shame or guilt experiences are better left buried in the past. As a result, we often develop a distorted self-image. Seeing ourselves in a negative light, we become critical of ourselves. Then we falsely believe that when bad things happen to us, we deserve them. We see ourselves as victims, accepting as fact that we deserve the bad treatment we get.

This falsehood can lead to any number of addictions, because we are trying to cover up the holes in our lives. We feel so badly about ourselves we will do anything to help assuage the pain that never goes away. Besides addictions, unresolved shame can lead to self-pity (victim mentality), inhibitions in behaviour, or even angry defiance—all designed to keep this sense of shame at bay. The emotional energy needed to keep the "shame door locked" is enormous. Then we wonder why we are so tired all the time.

When children suffer this sense of shame on an ongoing basis, the only way they can survive is to try to adapt to the adult world they live in. Their way of adapting is allowing people (parents, other adults, or peers) to continue to victimize them. Children will develop a false sense of identity to hide from the shame feelings that are stirring within. Although this false mask is designed to protect them from feeling more shame, it fails to work. They work hard at keeping the "shame door" closed because they are ashamed of their shame.

A good analogy between this behaviour and the world of nature can be seen. Citrus fruit growing in a topical climate like Florida will react to a sudden turn in cold temperatures. Grapefruits, oranges, and lemons will grow a thicker covering to protect the fruit inside when cold weather strikes. We do much the same. We develop "thicker skin" to protect the hurt and pain inside.

Characteristics of Unresolved Shame

Now is a good time to skip to Appendix 4 to do an exercise. It is entitled "Characteristics Seen in Adults Who Were Shamed in Childhood." Many of us believe that time will heal these wounds and that they eventually will "scab" and disappear. As I stated previously, time does not heal the pain of shame. Time simply pushes pain further down in the unconscious so we cannot deal with it effectively. But it doesn't go away; it waits to surface when another crisis occurs in our lives.

Doing this exercise will give you some objective sense as to whether or not you are dealing with unresolved shame issues. Typically, these issues will be ongoing in your lives and not one-time incidents. If you discover you have more shame issues than you realized, then make a commitment to get help in working out these things. (By the way, some of you will struggle with doing the exercise because it means confronting your shame. Try to be as honest as you can when you do the exercise or it will not be helpful to you.)

If these characteristics in the life of an adult are persistent, it will indicate that there are hidden areas of childhood shame that as yet have not been exposed. Wherever we are not living in freedom from the past, we are not functioning fully as God intended. The exercise is not designed to make you feel badly or ashamed, but to let you know your shame issues that need to be examined. My counselling goal is to surface issues in the unconscious and work on those areas so you can be free.

CHAPTER 22

CONNECTING ADULT SHAME
WITH ITS CHILDHOOD ROOTS

Many adults have lived with shame so long that they are at home in their feelings of inferiority, insecurity, or inadequacy—called shame. When they are challenged, their response is to say, "That's just the way I am" (often with the unspoken, "so please leave me alone"). It is true that we want to accept people as they are. However, a defensive response is usually an indication that they have something to hide. Not dealing with shame is unhealthy. To continue repressing these unresolved issues only leads to further troubles in the future.

When we live with a shamed-based set of behaviours, we are robbed of the freedom to discover who we really are and what God wants us to be. With unresolved shame in our lives, we are not free to become what God has called us to be. Shame-based behaviours from childhood explain why an abused wife consistently will go back to a husband abusing her. She even will return at the risk of her life! Why? Because she still operates in a victim mentality and unconsciously believes she deserves violent treatment. Sometimes a wife believes she is trying to rescue her husband. She will go back into the abusive situation believing that she can save her husband. "Nobody understands him like I do," she says.

When a man allows his boss to abuse him, not standing up for himself, he falsely believes he is unworthy of respect. I counselled a man who was apprenticing as a carpenter. He told me how his boss mistreated him day after day. I asked him how he could be more assertive speaking to his boss. Had he considered that it was time to change jobs? I suggested a number of strategies to help solve these daily pressures.

Each time I suggested an option, he had a reason it wouldn't work with his boss. Eventually he stopped coming to see me. I found out from mutual friends that it took him two years to leave this job. I also discovered that his father was a driven man, constantly pushing his son to achieve. Therefore, the son was accustomed to being treated poorly. At the same time, the son was desperately trying to prove to his father that he wasn't a quitter and that he could stick it out. However, the real issue was that the son was raised in a shame-based family but couldn't recognize it because shame was all he had known.

Persons living this way are likely functioning from a family system in which childhood shame issues have not been resolved. The childhood issues from a domineering shame-based parent will repeat themselves years later in adult life. In order to deal with adult shame, we must allow the "door of the shame closet" to be opened to examine the unresolved pain.

Opening the "Shame Door"

I am aware of the difficulty for most adults to open their "shame door." In the years I was employed at a counselling centre, I often felt that I could only get so far with my clients before they shut the door on me. Initially, I was puzzled by their refusal to dig deeper. I wanted to find out what was so fearful that they didn't want me to "go there." When I studied shame in the Bible, I began to understand the power of shame over people.

As I have said before, the difficulty is that we are deeply ashamed of our shame. How do you "open the door to shame" when you are too ashamed to acknowledge that you have hidden shame issues from your past? One of my goals for writing this book is to dare to talk about shame. I'm saying to you, "Look, it's all right to open the 'door of shame' and explore." Having shame issues is normal. Feeling vulnerable about them is all right. Seeking healing for hidden shame is okay.

I realized over the years of teaching this topic that I must be vulnerable myself to show others that exploring shame is not as frightening as it seems. I purposely have been vulnerable with you about my life to encourage you to open the "door" a crack.

I believe we must open the door to our hidden shame if we want to find the freedom in our lives that the Bible says is ours in Christ. Galatians 5:1 says: "It is for freedom that Christ has set us free. Stand firm, then, and do not let yourselves be burdened again by a yoke of slavery." As long as we are full of unresolved shame, I guarantee that we won't be able to live in the fullness of the Holy Spirit.

Shame can lead us either into HUMILITY or HUMILIATION. Humility accepts the fact that we have unhealed shame areas in our past. The alternative to not opening our hearts to deal with these issues is to live in humiliation. Either we learn from our past mistakes and become teachable or we will go back into hiding and say, "I'd prefer to remain in a safe place because security is more important to me than being open and taking the risk of humility."

Dealing with the Shame of Shame

When I went through my "dark night of the soul" in my late thirties (when our church split), I recall how raw I felt many times. I was ashamed at what had happened to the church because I saw myself as a failure as the leader. I remember my discomfort when Duane Harder came to deal with the pertinent issues in my life that needed work. At times I just didn't want him to come anymore, because I was certain something else in my life would be dredged up.

But every time Duane came, I knew I had to make a choice. Will I open up to him or will I fake it and tell him that I was doing all right? Although a struggle, somehow, by the grace of God, I humbled myself. All of us have to decide what we are going to do about the "shame door."

Isaiah 54:4–8 (NIV) speaks to this very issue. This is God's invitation to deal with our shame.

4 "Do not be afraid; you will not be put to shame.
  Do not fear disgrace; you will not be humiliated.
  You will forget the shame of your youth
    and remember no more the reproach of your widowhood.
5 For your Maker is your husband—
    the Lord Almighty is his name—
  the Holy One of Israel is your Redeemer;

he is called the God of all the earth.
6   The Lord will call you back
    as if you were a wife deserted and distressed in spirit—
    a wife who married young,
    only to be rejected," says your God.
7   "For a brief moment I abandoned you,
    but with deep compassion I will bring you back.
8   In a surge of anger
    I hid my face from you for a moment,
    but with everlasting kindness
    I will have compassion on you,"
    says the Lord your Redeemer.

In the Old Testament, a redeemer was one who purchased someone from the slave market. One of the stories of redemption in the Bible is the story of Hosea and his wife, Gomer. God asked Hosea to marry Gomer, even though she was a prostitute. Later, she left him and went back to her life of prostitution. God asked Hosea again, as a picture of His everlasting love for Israel, to go down to the slave market and purchase (redeem) his own wife.

In the message of Isaiah 54, God is saying that He will always go after us because of His love. But we have to make a choice to respond to His overture of love and redemption. We are afraid of being humiliated, but God says we will not be humiliated if we humble ourselves and respond to the redemptive work that He does in our lives. Father God has great compassion for us.

Isaiah 50:7 (NIV): "Because the Sovereign Lord helps me, I will not be disgraced. Therefore have I set my face like flint, and I know I will not be put to shame." Our hearts must determine that we will walk in the way God set for us. We all have unhealed shame in our pasts. By the grace of God, I continue to work on my issues.

Coping with Shame

The problem is not that we have unhealed negative shame but that we have chosen to live in this shame while coping with it rather than wanting it out. Wanting shame out is not an easy choice to make. Shame's power is extremely pervasive. Examining our shame is frightening, especially for men. But remember, all of us have a choice to make. The choice, in this case, is between humility and humiliation.

In humility we dare to examine our lives for what needs healing and cleansing. Behind the "shame door" might be unresolved anger and bitterness, or unresolved fear and anxiety issues. Perhaps guilt or shame issues in our past need to be brought to the cross for repentance and cleansing. There might be lies like inferiority, insecurity, or inadequacy that need repentance.

When we make the choice to deal with these hidden areas of shame, we become amazingly free people. Afterward, we can take the message of freedom to other people. I am exactly modeling this point. Because I have found my freedom, I delight in bringing the message of freedom to you. We not only know that we can come to that place of freedom, but also we know how to help others walk in freedom.

I'm going to pray a prayer of preparation for freedom; if you feel you are ready, please pray along with me.

Father, I'm making a decision today to commit myself to humility as a way out of my shame.

I relinquish my pride that covers my insecurity and reject negative shame as a hiding place.
I'm here to do business with You, Father.
Thank you, Father, for accepting me in all my shame and weakness. Amen.

If you just prayed that prayer, believe Father God has heard the sincerity of your heart; He will help you walk out the commitment you made. I encourage you to tell at least one other person what you have prayed. That's one more way of overcoming the control that shame had on you.

An Exercise for Your Development

Write out one memory of shame from your childhood that you are willing to share with others (it will have to be something that is not overwhelming or you will find it very difficult to share). The purpose of this exercise is to open the past by acknowledging your need to touch at least one childhood shame issue for healing purposes.

PART 5

BREAKING THE POWER
OF NEGATIVE SHAME

CHAPTER 23

THE POWER OF
NEGATIVE SHAME

Although I cannot say categorically, yet I believe that negative shame well may be the most powerful emotion that Satan uses against us to hold control over our lives. I am well aware that negative fear is a highly powerful emotion as well. So is repressed anger in all of its forms. But I believe that shame is the "master emotion." Although not a Biblical statement, my study of shame in the Bible leads me to agree with the expression used in psychology.

Shame as an emotional signal is not the real problem. The real problem is what lies behind the "shame door" that is hidden from us. Because of its power, negative shame can so control us that we are unable to obey God in certain areas. As we noted earlier, God uses positive shame to prevent us from falling into sin. But negative shame can have such power that we never experience life in the Spirit as God intended.

In the arena of shame, a tug of war is ongoing. The enemy uses our shame against us by causing us to feel ashamed of our sin, so we never work it through to redemption. Who among us reading this book can claim to have no sin or no failures in their lives? We all are in the same condition. When we are encouraged to examine our shame secrets, we can be healed. However, at the same time, we immediately are held captive by the fear of acknowledging our shame.

Shame Is Still an Issue

All of us still feel some areas of shame in our lives. We don't like aspects of our personalities, physical appearances, and relational abnormalities. In other words, we feel ashamed about ourselves. Then we do whatever we have to do to hide that from others. We are imprisoned in certain areas of our lives and do not want others to know about our "secrets."

If you doubt the power of negative shame, you will discover its power when you share one of your deep, dark secrets, past or present, in a public forum. I dare you to ride on public transportation and yell out an area of shame that you want to keep hidden. You can't do it. This is true for all of us. I'm no different from any of you: I couldn't do it, either. This example gives us an "inkling" about the power of negative shame. The fear of exposing shame overwhelms us.

However, God's desire is that we work on these shame issues so they no longer control us, or have mastery over our lives. God wants to turn what the enemy uses against us to work for us. That is, God wants to turn our negative shame into positive shame. He wants us to learn to use positive shame as boundaries that set us free from the power of sin in our lives. God takes what Satan has been using against us and uses it to establish a clear difference between right and wrong. These positive boundaries help us make daily decisions to live in God's right ways.

The first step in defeating the power of negative shame is to dare to open the "door of shame" and acknowledge that we have unhealed shame areas in our lives.

Shame—the Closed Door

Naturally—and I could say healthy in one sense—we want to protect any area of our lives that has been wounded, both in a physical sense as well as in an emotional or spiritual sense. Let me illustrate: when I was about ten years old, I attended a boys' summer camp in Point Roberts, Washington, US, with my twin brother, Grant.

One day, we were playing baseball. I played the short stop position between the second and third basemen. One of the boys on the other team, who was up to bat, hit the softball in the air into the infield. The second baseman, the third baseman, and I all tried to catch the ball to put the batter out. I suppose we were all trying to be the hero by catching this "pop fly."

As we ran to catch the ball without looking at each other, the other two boys crashed into me (I don't remember if we actually caught the ball). Because I was in the middle, I got squeezed between the other two. Immediately, I felt that something hurt in my shoulder. Of course, as a boy, I can't dare acknowledge anything wrong. I tried to stay in the game but my shoulder was really hurting. My left arm, in particular, seemed to lose some of its strength.

Later in the day, I went to the camp nurse and told her something was wrong with my collarbone. She examined me but could not see anything wrong except what I told her about my collarbone being sore. She did, however, put my left arm in a sling (mostly, I suspect, to placate me, because she thought I was being rather whiny). The next day when all the campers went on a hike, I had difficulty keeping up. I went back to the nurse later that day to tell her something was definitely wrong. She dismissed me again, maybe thinking I was a bit homesick. I survived the rest of my time at camp but I knew something did not feel right.

When I got home I told my mother, who had been a nurse for eighteen years; she knew medical issues. She felt my shoulder, saw my pain, and decided I needed an X-ray. The X-ray revealed that I had a "green stick" fracture. The shoulder bone was not completely broken but was fractured. The next week we went back to this camp to pick up my younger brother, Ross. Of course, I proudly walked into the nurse's station to show her that she was wrong not to have taken more pity on me.

Normally, when an area of our body is wounded, we protect it with special care. During the rest of the camp, I often held my left arm with my right arm to help immobilize it. In the physical realm, if we refuse to allow the doctor to examine the soreness because it hurts so much, we inhibit the doctor from helping us heal.

Protecting Our Wounds Is Normal

Emotionally, the same is true. We want to protect areas of our lives that have been wounded—that is normal. But when a professional tries to help us deal with our emotional wounds and we push him away, we are working against ourselves. When a doctor wants to examine our physical wounds and we push him away, we would admit that doesn't make sense. The same is true in the soul. When we push away a person trying to help, it is counterproductive to healing. Of course it hurts; that is the very reason we need to deal with it.

That's what negative shame does. It acts as a barrier; a closed door. When issues in our lives need to be examined for emotional healing, we must be aware of the power of negative shame that wants to keep that "door" closed. Before painful areas of our lives can be examined and healed, we must find a way to crack the "door" open. We must let the healing light of Jesus Christ expose the darkness hidden in our lives.

Satan has used the power of negative shame against human beings back to the Garden of Eden. When Adam and Eve sinned against God, Genesis 3 says that they hid themselves from God because they felt ashamed. Satan has been telling that lie ever since. Satan tells us it is better to hide from God than let His light shine on sin and shame .Why is hiding sin better? "Because God will reject you," says Satan. However, the guilt signal is designed by God to bring attention to an area of wrong that needs correction. When the guilt signal gets buried behind the "closed door of shame," we won't allow the Holy Spirit to bring correction and healing.

The Poverty Spirit

Years ago when I was pastoring our church, a couple of my friends who were elders on our leaders' team "dared" to confront me with an area in my life that needed to be addressed. Both John and Mike saw a "poverty spirit" operating in me that I could not see. They met with me to talk about what they saw in me. They were concerned with how

I handled my finances in certain areas. What they picked up about me was that I would sometimes hint that I wasn't paid enough as the pastor of the church. I was partially paid by what I earned at the counselling centre and partially supported by the church. They also saw some other financial issues in my life.

Rather than valuing this help, I received it as accusation (in my insecurity). I reacted with anger because it felt to me like an attack. We began an argument that wasn't resolved because I wasn't open to their feedback. Finally, to close the conversation, I told them (although I didn't believe they were right) I would ask God to show me if what they saw was true. Of course I knew they were wrong, so I didn't expect the Holy Spirit to show me anything (just a little bit of pride in the way, eh).

That weekend, our family travelled with our friends, Doug and Bobbi, from our church for a holiday getaway. I did pray (rather casually), "Lord, if You have something that I need to see, show me." Of course, I wasn't expecting Him to show me anything. However, on the weekend, on four separate occasions, the Holy Spirit showed me clearly that I was dealing with a poverty spirit. (This experience provided me with an opportunity to humble myself before my fellow leaders, receive deliverance prayer, and move on to more freedom in this area of my life.)

A poverty spirit is a mental attitude directed by a demonic force that tells people that God will not provide adequately for them. It robs them of their faith, because they fail to trust God for provision; it subsequently prevents God from blessing them. The poverty spirit blocks God's people from receiving His blessings which, in turn, stops these blessings from being passed on to others to bring them to God. (See Appendix 5 for a list of the ways this poverty spirit can manifest itself.)

Looking back, I believe I developed this poverty spirit through a vow I made when I was in college and university—that I would graduate not owing the bank or government a lot of money. As a result of that vow, I carefully watched how I spent every dime. I lived frugally (and miserly, too) so I wouldn't get into debt. In fact, after ten years of postsecondary education, I had accumulated only $950 in debt, which Sherry and I paid off during our first year of marriage.

When I was single, living this way was somewhat manageable. But after I married and had a family, it created tension in our relationship. When money was short, I would hint to the elders team that we were not adequately paid. Those complaints were what Mike and John noticed that concerned them. (By the way, when I returned from that weekend, I asked Mike and John to pray to release me from that poverty spirit. Since that time, I have had much more freedom [not perfect for sure] in the area of trusting God for His provision for our family.)

For me, part of the issue was shame when John and Mike pointed out a weakness in my life. They started the discussion with me very graciously. They did not accuse me of a poverty spirit. I felt ashamed that someone else had to point it out to me.

The Sensitivity of Shame Issues

When someone close to us tries to help us see areas of unresolved bitterness, fear, insecurity, or guilt, we feel shamed for having unresolved issues in our lives; we react defensively. We defend ourselves and our behaviour or lifestyle and are afraid of hearing negatives about ourselves. In counselling, I have to carefully listen to the Holy Spirit when I am touching areas of shame with my counsellee. I need to hear the

Holy Spirit saying to me now is the time to discuss it. Even then, I must approach the subject cautiously.

If we are closed to hearing what others see in us, the only other option is to try to resolve issues on our own. Thus, when we see sin, failure or dysfunction in our lives, we will try to forgive ourselves (as I shared earlier in the book). Self-forgiveness (because we feel ashamed) nullifies the work of the cross. We reject the salvation that Jesus accomplished for us on the cross by His substitutionary death when we think we can forgive ourselves.

Trying to Forgive Ourselves

Let me say emphatically once again: **WE CANNOT FORGIVE OURSELVES!** No place does the Bible state we are able to forgive ourselves. People frequently use the phrase, "You've got to forgive yourself." But self-forgiveness is not Biblically correct. In fact, I think it is one of the most insidious lies that Satan has ever used. If we can forgive ourselves, we don't need the work of Christ accomplishing what He did on the cross. Forgiving ourselves is humanism at its core.

I understand what people are trying to express by needing to forgive themselves. But it means they have not received God's forgiveness for their sin. Because they have not humbled themselves to acknowledge that only God can forgive, they falsely try to forgive themselves. To think I can forgive myself becomes pride.

Let me give an illustration that may help you understand this with clarity. Suppose a police officer charged you with a driving offense and you decide to fight the charge. You stand before the judge as he reads the offense. When he asks you for your plea, you say, "Guilty, your honour." But you tell him not to worry about it because you have decided to forgive yourself. Somewhat incredulously, the judge looks you straight in the eye and tells you that you don't have the authority in his court to forgive yourself.

As we stand before Almighty God, we don't have the authority to forgive ourselves. However, if we are willing to acknowledge our guilt (confession), we can receive God's mercy and forgiveness. Sometimes we don't receive God's forgiveness because we don't think we are worthy. Other times we choose not to receive God's forgiveness because we don't think we need it. Like Adam and Eve in the Garden of Eden, we have become our own "gods." Based on that false premise, we think we are able to forgive ourselves.

However, in reality, we can **receive** forgiveness only from someone who has authority to forgive. Jesus suffered and died on the cross because we can't forgive ourselves. When we try to, we are mixing grace and works. Ephesians 2: 8–9 states, "For it is by grace you have been saved, through faith—and this is not from yourselves, it is the gift of God—not by works, so that no one can boast." If we could forgive ourselves, then who needs Jesus?

Fix Our Eyes on Jesus

Hebrews 12:2 (NIV) tells us to "fix our eyes on Jesus, the author and perfecter of our faith, who for the joy set before him endured the cross, scorning its shame, and sat down at the right hand of God." Death by crucifixion was the most humiliating and excruciating form of punishment in the Roman Empire. They not only killed their enemies but they did it in the most shameful way possible. The person hanging on a Roman cross was naked. The execution was designed to shame publically the criminal in every way possible. The physical torture was one punishment, but the shame was another way to punish the person.

If you are living under the power of negative shame because of your ignorance, then you can ask God to change you. But once aware of the choice, you must either believe or not believe God's way of salvation; accordingly you are without excuse. You choose either to humble yourself before God in this life, or you experience humiliation when you stand before Him on Judgment Day.

When we fear being exposed for all the sin in our lives, we live under the power of negative shame. We believe a lie that God's forgiveness and love won't cover all our sins or that some of our sins are too great for the grace of God. Satan loves to trick us with that lie. "My sin is too great or too horrendous to be forgiven."

CHAPTER 24

THE PLACE OF
THE CROSS IN SHAME

Romans 1:16 (NIV): "I am not ashamed of the gospel, because it is the power of God for the salvation of everyone who believes: first for the Jew, then for the Gentile." I believe Paul means that we often are ashamed of the wrong thing. Why did the Holy Spirit direct Paul to write this verse from a negative perspective? "I am NOT ashamed of the gospel…." I think what he is saying is that we are often more ashamed of the gospel and the "weakness" of the cross than we are ashamed of our own sin. So Paul says, "I am not ashamed of the gospel" because he knew its power to free people from a life of slavery to sin.

If we were to put these two issues (the gospel versus our sin) on a balance scale, we could see which has more weight or influence in our lives. Is it the power of the gospel to change us or the shame in our lives which still controls us?

Let me express Romans 1:16 from the positive perspective instead of the negative perspective. "I confess and acknowledge **openly and**

gladly that the gospel is the power of God for the salvation of everyone who believes…. (my translation)" Paul is saying that the power of the gospel far exceeds the power of shame. However, we tend to believe the lie that the power of shame is much greater than the power of the gospel.

We have to truly believe Romans 1:16 if we are to open the "door of shame." We must believe that the power of the gospel is much greater than the power of negative shame. I believe that many of us know this truth intellectually but not experientially. All our lives we will be in need of the gospel to heal and change us. If we don't believe this, we will attempt to make changes in our lives by "doing" rather than "believing." The gospel then becomes a gospel of works rather than a gospel received by faith.

We know only one path into the Kingdom of God. But as time goes by, we slip into a gospel of works when maintaining our sanctification and maturing in our walk with Jesus. We believe we have to do something to please God rather than believe that when we surrender to the Holy Spirit's direction each day, He will direct us and live in us.

Overcoming Shame Issues by "Doing"

Perhaps that's the reason so many Christians struggle with areas of addiction, because of trying to overcome shame issues by "doing" rather than by coming to the cross with our confession each day. Are we aware of how much emotional energy we use trying to overcome our shame? Some of this effort at overcoming even gets falsely considered as ministry for the Kingdom of God. Many well-meaning Christians and Christian leaders try to overcome shame by serving God. Our drivenness gets in the way of what God is doing in His Kingdom. We try to overcome our hidden shame by "doing."

When we follow this cycle, we nullify the work of the cross. The cross is a place of death. At the cross we die to self-determination, self-will, and self-effort. We can't overcome shame issues in our lives through self-effort. When we try, we find ourselves in various forms of addiction. The only way to defeat shame is with the power of the cross. God already has done all the work of overcoming shame through Jesus' death on the cross. Faith allows us to receive what God has done through the cross.

Isaiah 53: 3–6 (NIV) gives us the perspective we need. Look at what Jesus has done for us. He has done it all so we don't have to attempt to find our own salvation.

3   He was despised and rejected by men,
    a man of suffering, and familiar with suffering.
    Like one from whom men hide their faces
    he was despised, and we esteemed him not.
4   Surely he took up our infirmities
    and carried our sorrows,
    yet we considered him stricken by God,
    smitten by him, and afflicted.
5   But he was pierced for our transgressions,
    he was crushed for our iniquities;
    the punishment that brought us peace was on him,
    and by his wounds we are healed.
6   We all, like sheep, have gone astray,
    each of us has turned to his own way;
    and the Lord has laid on him
    the iniquity of us all.

These verses describe what Jesus went through for us to be brought back into relationship with a holy God. That's what was laid on Him so it wouldn't have to be laid on us. He took our shame so we wouldn't have to carry it. That's why only the substitutionary death of Jesus will remove both the stain of our shame and the power of the shame that keeps us locked up.

Jesus Has Done It All

We can be truly healed only by accepting what Jesus already has done on the cross for us. Jesus has done it all so we don't have to provide forgiveness for ourselves. I know many times I have tried to please God by doing things for Him, only to fail repeatedly. I finally concluded that nothing I could do would please God, except to accept what Jesus had already done. Then I would say, "Thank you for your forgiveness, Jesus; I receive your cleansing again."

In receiving His work on the cross and believing it is complete, we find freedom. We can bring anything behind the "shame door" to Him in confession and see it resolved. Some of you have been Christians for so long that you may have forgotten how to appropriate this truth on an ongoing basis. Although we know this truth, we are not practicing it.

Only one place finds release from the deep pains of life—the cross. The cross also provides forgiveness for our "unforgiveable" shame. All our sins can be forgiven, but when we don't believe this, we hide them. Sometimes we think we have gone too far in our sin and falsely believe we have "out-sinned" the grace of God.

I remember as a young man attending the University of Calgary. I was struggling with an issue of lust. I looked at the lovely young ladies on campus with impure thoughts. I knew this sin of lust was wrong, but I kept falling into it. On this particular day, I remember going through this struggle seven times, giving in to lust. I felt so ashamed of myself. I said there was no more forgiveness for me. The enemy robbed me of the joy of my salvation.

I went home to the place I was boarding to have tears over my sin and shame. Then I noticed a book on my bookshelf someone had given me, but I had not yet read. Entitled *Love is Now* by Pete Gilquist, I started reading that book feeling like it was written specifically for me. He said the forgiveness of God is unconditional; you can't "outsin" the grace of God. I "ate up" the book, so to speak. I realized the lie that I had accepted and immediately received God's forgiveness and cleansing for my sin.

Shame had brought me to a standstill. I falsely believed there was no more forgiveness for me. That's a lie; I suspect that all of us have fallen into this lie many times.

Faith Is Spelled "Risk" and "Rest"

I've personally heard the late John Wimber, founder of the Vineyard movement speak a number of times. One of the quotes I remember from him was: "How to you spell faith?" And his answer always was: "r-i-s-k." I like that notion because faith has an element of stepping outside our comfort zones and "risking" new adventures of faith in the Kingdom—no risk, no adventure.

However, another way to spell faith is "r-e-s-t." Both are valid ways to spell faith. In fact, there are probably several more ways to spell faith. How about "s-e-e-i-n-g" or "h-e-a-r-i-n-g"? But I digress. Why do I say we can spell faith, "r-e-s-t"? Because Hebrews 4 makes a clear statement about faith and rest. Hebrews 4:1–2; 6–11 (NIV):

1   Therefore, since the promise of entering his rest still stands, let us be careful that none of you be found to have fallen short of it.

2   For we also have had the gospel preached to us as they did but the message they heard was of no value to them, because those who heard it did not combine it with faith.

6   It still remains that some will enter that rest, those who formerly had the gospel preached to them did not go in because of their disobedience,

7   Therefore, God again set a certain day, calling it Today, when a long time later he spoke through David, as was said before:
        "Today, if you hear his voice,
        do not harden your hearts."

8   For if Joshua had given them rest, God would not have spoken later about another day.

9   There remains, then, a Sabbath-rest for the people of God;

10 for anyone who enters God's rest also rests from his work, just as God did from his.

11 Let us, therefore, make every effort to enter that rest, so that no one will fall by following their example of disobedience.

The disobedience to which the writer of Hebrews refers to is a return to a gospel of works after the believer has entered the Kingdom by faith alone. One of the major challenges to overcoming the power of shame is trying—through our own efforts, through a gospel of works. The power of shame is much greater than our personal strength. But the power of shame pales in comparison to the power of the gospel. When we use the power of the gospel, we can defeat shame.

Jesus Was Crucified in Shame

When we choose to lock the "closet of shame" in our lives, we are saying, in essence, "I will take care of my own shame by keeping it hidden. Hiding is the only way I know how to deal with shame." But Jesus took our shame on Himself when He died on the cross. He hung on the cross naked and exposed, totally shamed, so we wouldn't have to face our own shame. I realize that most pictures of Jesus on the cross have Him wearing a loincloth (and I understand that prudence), but he was fully exposed and shamed so we won't have to be exposed.

The good news about Jesus taking on our shame is fulfilled when we confess our sin and shame to Jesus, repenting of the lie that caused the sin. Confession is such a gift from God to deal with our shame. When we confess it privately to God and to a trusted person, and have the power of forgiveness pronounced over us, we are set free of the "tentacles" of shame.

When we open the "door" of our hearts to Jesus, He will shine His light to expose the darkness. We are saying to Jesus, "You are right about what you have seen in my heart but I know that you won't hold it against me, because You totally have forgiven me." Our confession is our agreement with Jesus' perspective of the truth about our hearts. Agreeing with Jesus' perspective is what sets us free.

I suggest we confess our shame to another person that we trust so we can hear, from a human perspective, that our sin is cleansed and our shame is released. When we confess our shame to another person, he can pronounce forgiveness in the authority of Jesus' name. I have heard many people's confessions and observed how free they become afterward.

The Cleansing Forgiveness of Father God

Are you living in the total freedom that Christ purchased for you on the cross? Freedom isn't found in just opening the "door of shame." Freedom is found in receiving the cleansing forgiveness of Father God. Romans 9:30–33 (NIV) clarifies the power of confession in dealing with shame.

30 "What then shall we say? That the Gentiles, who did not pursue righteousness, have obtained it, a righteousness that is by faith

31 but Israel, who pursued a law of righteousness, has not obtained it.

32 Why not? Because they pursued it not by faith but as it were by works. They stumbled over the stumbling stone.

33 As it is written, "See I lay in Zion a stone that causes men to stumble, a rock that makes them fall. The one who trusts in him will never be put to shame."

The person who **trusts** in Jesus is set free of his or her shame. Not by "doing" all kinds of things (or hiding our shame) are we free. By trusting the finished work of Jesus on the cross, we are set free. When we lock the "door of shame" in our lives, we not only lock out other people but also we lock that door to Jesus. The truth of this Scripture in Romans is so crucial that the Holy Spirit placed it in the Bible four times. It initially appears in Isaiah 28:16 and it is repeated in Romans 9:33, Romans 10:11, and 1 Peter 2:6.

CHAPTER 25

PUTTING SHAME INTO WORDS

In order for the power of shame to be broken, we must speak out the dark secrets in our lives. To be free from the power of shame we have to confess the shame of the past, but we must do it without creating more shame. Sharing one's shame secrets is extremely sensitive. If someone forces us to open the "shame door," it creates more shame. If we feel coerced into sharing our shame, then later we will regret feeling forced to open that "door." We may then make a vow to never do that again.

If someone dares to open his or her "shame door" in your presence, you must treat him with the utmost sensitivity. You must provide such people a safe haven when they are so vulnerable. When the "terrible truth" is spoken out (and it often isn't as terrible as we think), there must not be any hint of condemnation or rejection.

One woman I counselled initially came to see me because of low self-esteem and other issues in her marriage. I don't think she was a born-again believer, but she was a regular church attender. As she was working through issues with me, one day she told me she had a friend who had gone through two abortions and she wondered how to help her. As soon as she told me that, the Holy Spirit told me that she was the one who had the abortions. I gave her some direction to help her "friend" deal with the unconfessed guilt of the abortions.

The next time she came to see me for counselling she said, "I have something to say to you. The 'friend' who had the two abortions was really me." I told her I already knew that but I thanked her sincerely for the honesty of her confession. I asked her if she wanted me to help her deal with her guilt and she said yes. So I had her confess her guilt to me (with lots of tears) and I extended the forgiveness of Jesus to her.

After a few more counselling sessions, she told me she had another confession to make. She said, "I haven't had two abortions—I've had five. The first two were under pressure from my father because I was a young teenager at the time. But the last three were my choice." At that point, she wept deeply for quite a while at the relief of finally touching her shame. The reason that she told me about the "friend" who had had the two abortions was because she was testing me to see how I would react to abortion.

She knew I was a pastor as well as a psychologist. She wanted to see how I would handle her "terrible truth." When she saw that I offered compassion not condemnation, she chose to tell me the truth about the first two abortions, then tell about the other three abortions. She had been carrying this pain of unconfessed guilt for many years—significantly affecting her self-esteem, her marriage, and her physical health. I was delighted to represent Jesus to her (John 8:1–11).

No Condemnation

If we are going to hear people's shame confessions, we have to be unshockable. For people to be set free of their guilt and shame, they have to trust that Jesus will not only forgive them but He will not condemn them either. In this same way, we have to be "Jesus" to people who want to deal with their shame and not condemn them, especially when they share so vulnerably. We must be mature enough in our relationship with Jesus to be able to handle the "terrible truth" that they share with us.

Father God wants us to get free. He wants to break the hold that Satan has had on us through our shame. He wants us to deal with the enormous fear of rejection that resides in all of us. What breaks the power of shame is that we can share our deep, dark secrets and be accepted in the process. This is what every one of us seeks: unconditional acceptance that breaks the power of shame. **The power behind negative shame is the fear of rejection.**

We all are afraid to share our secrets because we think, *If you find out such and such about me, you will never want anything to do with me. If you don't reject me outright, I know you won't like me or want to be around me.*

I want to share something immensely personal for me right now. Not that I want to share it, but I believe the Holy Spirit wants me to be vulnerable in my writing so you understand I am not just discussing the theory of dealing with shame but the reality of having experienced it myself.

Working through My Own Shame Issues

Years ago when I first started putting together the material on shame for the workshop I have since taught many times, I struggled with a personal issue of shame that kept getting in my way. I was twenty-two years old when I met Sherry, who later became my wife. She was fifteen years old and part of the youth group for which I was the youth pastor. I had just ended a serious relationship in Bible College in which I had asked a young lady to marry me; she wisely refused.

When I moved to Calgary, Alberta, I attended a Baptist church. I noticed this cute young girl but I had sworn off females; and she was too young. However, within about four months I knew that I was eventually going to marry Sherry (at her age, she certainly didn't have the same sense). A few months later I did ask her parents for permission to begin a careful relationship with her because it was becoming apparent in the youth group that the youth pastor was sweet on this particular girl.

So when I was twenty-six and Sherry was eighteen, we were married. Although I had quite a history of relationships with young ladies, I was the first boyfriend that Sherry ever had. Over the early years of our marriage, I had been very cautious about sharing much of my girlfriend history with Sherry. I told her that she didn't need to be bothered with my former relationships because it was past history. I had told her the names of my many girlfriends but I never told her about what went on with them. I felt ashamed of my past.

I grew up in a good evangelical Christian home, attending a Baptist church during those years. Our pastor, Doug Harris, regularly spoke on holiness and encouraged the youth in the church to live in sexual purity. He lived his message with integrity, so I never saw his encouragement for holy living as religious pressure. He did not pressure us, but he called us regularly to live holy lives.

However, despite his encouragement, some of our youth group lived a double life in this area of sexual purity, and I was one of them. Looking back, I can remember many times making trips to the "altar" to confess my sin and then going back to the same behaviour in a week or so. As Doug Harris preached many messages on sexual purity and living righteously, I was convicted for a while, but I had a strong need to be accepted by my peers so it didn't last long. Part of the shame for me was that I knew better, but I violated my own conscience.

My Wonderful Wife

I was a virgin when I married Sherry, but that was because of the mercy and grace God gave to me. I realize from the many stories of sexual pain and dysfunction I have heard over the years that my story may seem quite tame. But the shame for me was that I knew better. My wife is a beautiful woman, both inside and out. I am truly a blessed man to have married such a wonderful woman. But I did not honour her in the early years of our marriage, because I kept her out of this area of my past. Because I wouldn't let her into those areas of my life, she struggled at times with trusting me, as she didn't know fully what was in my past.

When I started researching material for the workshop on shame, I kept running into my own "shame demons." The Holy Spirit put His full focus on this area of shame. I couldn't handle it, so I stopped working on my research on shame. However, a little while later, I returned to developing the workshop, because I knew I was supposed to develop it. The "shame door" would be cracked open a little, but I couldn't handle it so I stopped again and again. This went on over a period of two years.

Sherry and I had a number of unresolved issues over this area of my vulnerability, because I continually wounded her by the fear I had of dealing with my shame. Of course, it affected the emotional intimacy in our relationship because I wouldn't let her into this area of my life. At one level I knew Sherry would never divorce me but at another unconscious level, I was so afraid of what her reaction would be if I opened up. I believed the lie that she would never be able to respect me truly if I shared my past. The power of shame was acutely strong in my life.

One day we were in a park in Lethbridge with our family and who should we meet but one of my old girlfriends. She was visiting Lethbridge to see an uncle and aunt and we ran into her and her husband. God had set me up! After that "chance" meeting, Sherry asked me about this past relationship. Again I skirted the issue, but I knew I couldn't keep putting it off.

Finally, the Holy Spirit spoke strongly to me telling me He wouldn't enable me to complete the workshop until I got the courage to talk with Sherry about this issue of shame. So I said to Sherry, "We need to talk." I had built up this issue to such an extent by putting it off for so many years.

One evening, we sat down after the children were in bed and I shared about my past relationships with her. I shared the details of all the things I had done that I was ashamed of. After confessing to her I asked her to forgive me, not only for what had happened in the past but also for how long it had taken me to be honest and vulnerable with her. (By the way, when I finished sharing everything, she said, "That's it?" Because I had held out so long, I had made a "mountain out of a molehill" in my mind.)

The power of shame was so enormous that I was not free in this area of my life. After my confession to Sherry, I felt as if someone had removed a hundred pounds off my back. It enabled us to live in greater and more delightful intimacy in our relationship. It also allowed me to get back to my shame research. It gave me a freedom with the Holy Spirit that I had not known fully before.

The Fear of Rejection

The fear of rejection is the primary reason we keep the "door of shame" closed in our lives. I know that as you are reading my story the "shame demons" in your lives are stirring and you are asking yourself, "Do I have the courage to face my shame issues?" Almost every time I have taught the Free To Be Me workshop, someone has asked me afterwards if they can tell me what they have never told anyone before. They ask because my vulnerability expresses I can be trusted to hear their shame secret without condemning them.

Once you find someone to trust, you find out that your "terrible truths" are not so overwhelming as you thought. Even if what you have in your past is devastating, God always provides a place to confess and receive the cleansing necessary for freedom. Because of my story, I love hearing other people's stories so I can help set them free, too. The power of the gospel is amazing. But to be set free, you have to trust "someone." Some people believe that their sin is unforgiveable, but as best as I can interpret Scripture, the only "unforgiveable sin" is attributing the work of Holy Spirit to the devil—Matthew 12:22–29 and Mark 3:20–30. In other words, there is only one sin that is so great it can't be forgiven.

Our willingness to express our shame breaks the hold shame has over us. When we are able to muster the courage to open the shame door, we are able to emerge from our own harsh, self-imposed rules and the enemy's lies about shame. We think we are protecting ourselves by keeping the door closed but the opposite is true. We are not free to enjoy the good news that we have been set completely free. The enemy will try to frighten us with a worst-case scenario to try to keep us locked up in our self-imposed prisons.

Coming out of Hiding

To come out of hiding and to be able to speak about our shame to a trusted person is a tremendously healing experience. I understand the fearfulness of being vulnerable enough to share major shame issues. Even in writing, I am aware that I don't want to manipulate readers to feel pressured to share their shame issues. Our confession must come from a conviction of wanting freedom more than wanting to conceal shame.

No one likes to admit he was wrong. Acknowledging wrong creates a great deal of insecurity in us, even when we think about it. We often equate being wrong or making mistakes to being rejected. By putting shame into words with a trusted companion, we are able to move past those damning emotions that control us. My desire is to give you a fresh, new perspective to examine shame, so you will take the risk of opening your heart.

Think about this question: **what if you could have an iron-clad**

guarantee that no matter what you shared, it would be forgiven and you would not be rejected? Would you do it? I expect the answer is yes. That proves we all are looking for a safe place with a trusted person to open our hearts. This is what it means to trust Jesus with our hearts, because we believe that He will not reject us or ever leave us because of our sin.

Trusting Jesus Is Hard

Romans 9 tells us that we often stumble over Jesus. We are more afraid to trust Jesus than we can admit. In the past when we trusted God's people, they have let us down. We reason that if God's people can hurt us, then God Himself can too. Even though as Christians we have often failed to be trustworthy, we still only have one option to get free. That is trusting Jesus with our confession and trusting God's people to represent Jesus well.

It is important to choose your "confidante" wisely. Some Christians can't handle hearing painful or difficult confessions. Other people don't know how to keep a confidence. Some people are not mature enough to handle other people's pain. But I do believe there are trustworthy, mature Christians who can handle your emotional pain. I know it takes great courage for the first step of being vulnerable, so choose your confidante following lots of prayer.

However, the alternative to remaining secretive is to pay an even higher price. The cost to our emotional systems and to our immune systems in keeping our "shame door" closed is exorbitant. We become fearful, shallow, inhibited, locked-up people who keep others from really knowing us because we are afraid to know ourselves. We won't fulfill our destinies. We won't have much of a testimony to share with others of the freedom Christ has given us. And we can bring significant health problems on ourselves because of our lowered immune systems.

If we Christians are going to help others find their freedom, we have to walk in our own freedom. I have written this book on finding freedom because I want people to imitate me, at least to the degree that I sound and look like Jesus. I have a passion to help people find freedom. I keep asking God for more areas of freedom for myself so I can give more to others. The only way to walk in freedom is to walk in the way of the cross. It means dying to yourself daily—dying to your pride, dying to your personal ambitions, dying to your fears, dying to the right to hold grudges, and dying to your shame.

Dying to ourselves is a way of saying, "Father God, I trust you." This trust is the way of the cross. The gospel of Jesus Christ is more powerful than the power of shame. I know it from the Word of God, but I also know it experientially.

CHAPTER 26

SHAME AND SECRETS

So, in saying that shame secrets need to be brought to the cross and worked out, does that mean that there is no place for secrets in our lives? I want to explore this potential contradiction with you so we avoid any confusion in our thinking. Secrets are a paradox—like a two-edged sword. Secrets both can save us and destroy us. They are like dynamite. Secrets can be used constructively or destructively. Understanding the value of secrets can help us distinguish between positive shame and negative shame.

Healthy Secrets

Let's check some places in the Bible that make reference to secrets.

Matthew 6:1–4 (NIV)

1 "Be careful not to do your acts of righteousness before men to be seen by them. If you do, you will have no reward from your Father in heaven.

2 "So when you give to the needy, do not announce it with trumpets, as the hypocrites do in the synagogues and on the streets, to be honored by men. I tell you the truth, they have received their reward in full.

3 But when you give to the needy, do not let your left hand know what your right hand is doing,

4 so that your giving may be in secret. Then your Father, who sees what is done in secret, will reward you.

Jesus goes on to give the same instruction about praying and fasting in secret. He commends us when we keep certain things secret. Jesus wants to protect us from falling into the trap of pride, which the Pharisees fell into when they thought they were doing good things for God. (See Matthew 6:1–18)

Sometimes God tells us to keep secrets because it is necessary to save our lives. One of the examples in the Bible that demonstrates this point, in a negative sense, is the story of Samson in the book of Judges. Samson's failure to keep secret the source of his great strength cost him his life (as well as his hair and his eyesight). When he was tricked by Delilah into telling her about the source of his strength, she went directly to his enemies, the Philistines, to share his secret with them. They gladly captured him and put out the eyes of their great enemy. (See Judges 16:5–6; 9: 5–17)

Esther is another Biblical example of the importance of keeping a secret. Esther's wise uncle, Mordecai, realized the danger of Esther being Jewish, even though she was the queen. When Haman decided to destroy all the Jewish people in the kingdom of Medo-Persia, even Esther was in danger of losing her life. Mordecai understood that the anti-Semitic feelings that Haman had stirred up put Esther's life in jeopardy. By keeping her ethnic background secret, she not only saved her own life but the lives of all the Jewish people (See Esther 2:20).

Jesus Himself kept certain secrets. As John records in his gospel in chapter 7, Jesus knew men's hearts and He was aware of the pressure coming from some people to reveal, prematurely, that He was the promised Messiah.

John 7:10 (NIV): "However, after his brothers had left for the Feast, he went also, not publicly but in secret." Jesus knew there were times to keep things secret. At this point in his life, Jesus' brothers did not believe in Him and they were quite willing to mock Him. They said to Jesus, taunting Him, "If you are such a public figure as the Messiah why are you trying to hide in secret." Jesus knew that it was not time to reveal too much about Himself. He was waiting for His Father's time.

Paul Tournier

In a book entitled *Secrets*, author Paul Tournier tells about the importance of secrets for one's healthy emotional development. He says, "*It is to the extent that [a child] has secrets from his parents that he gains an awareness of self; it is to the extent that he becomes free to keep his secrets from them that he gets an awareness of being distinct from them, of having his own individuality, of being a person."*

Please understand, first, what I am NOT saying. I am not saying that a child should be encouraged to keep secrets from his parents. I encourage children, especially young children, to share openly what's on their minds with their parents. However, as the child matures, he must be given the privilege of developing his own thought processes secretly, in order to mature enough to handle life on his own.

Tournier says that as children age, parents need to respect the child's right to privacy and being allowed to have secrets. Parents need wisdom as to when it is right to respect their children's need for private thoughts and when to insist that what he is hiding must be expressed because of danger to him. Interestingly, God respected Adam and Eve's right to hide in the Garden when they first sinned. God came to Adam and Eve, asking them questions. Although God already knew the answers, He wanted Adam and Eve to take ownership of their sin and rebellion. He could have forced them to reveal their secret of eating the forbidden fruit, but He chose to let them own their secret.

Individuating from Parents

As children grow into late adolescent years, they must individuate from their parents to gain emotional maturity. At some point, parents must allow their children to keep certain secrets from them. Of course parents must distinguish between healthy and unhealthy secrets. Many parents are threatened by the idea that they don't have access into every corner of their children's minds and hearts. They think that knowing everything about their children's thought lives will protect them and keep them from danger.

Think for a moment if you, as an adult, were not allowed to have any secrets. Every thought you have would be flashed on a tiny billboard on your forehead. Yikes! That scares every one of us. What if every motive we have for our behaviour were also publicly exposed? Just thinking about that possibility scares us. We know how much we value being able to have healthy secrets.

Even the clothes we wear allows us to keep secret that which only our spouses should see. In His wisdom, God has granted us secrets that are known only to Him. It is why the Holy Spirit quietly speaks to us in our hearts, to allow us to confess and deal with secrets that are destructive to us. But He doesn't force us to reveal them. He gently encourages us to acknowledge the secrets of our hearts that are self-destructive.

While it is true that some secrets can be healthy, it is also true that some can be destructive. What makes the crucial difference? It is how we deal with our guilt and shame issues.

Destructive Secrets

Healthy secrets are like beautiful wrapping paper around a precious gift. Destructive secrets are like a serial murderer, cloaked in shame, skulking around a neighbourhood looking for his next victim. An unimaginable power of fear associates with these secret ways. Negative shame often demands our agonized silence. When we live with destructive secrets, we are constantly trying to find ways to neutralize the "torture chamber" going on inside of us.

Over the years, I have heard many shame stories from individuals who grew up in families where family secrets had to be kept. I remember a time a man with a "secret" came to see me. The counselling session started out with him sharing what he felt safe. I could sense we were not quite hitting the "real" issue in his life. I knew that I needed to move carefully, because I sensed something significant in his past that he was hesitant to reveal.

When I asked him things about his father, he shared what he felt was safe. His father had died a few years earlier. I could sense a reluctance to volunteer more information, so I asked him how his father had died. At that point, I could see shame on his face. He finally told me that his father committed suicide. Then he told me that his father had been a pastor for many years. When his father chose to take his life, he caused great shame in the whole family.

Trying to be sensitive with this family secret, I could tell he had more. This young man had taken on himself the false guilt of contributing to his father's suicide by the way he lived. He had lived through a period of rebellion in earlier years. I suggested to him that he seemed to have taken on some of his father's "demons." Would he be interested in exploring this issue with me? He told me, quickly, that other counsellors had tried in the past, but the conversation never lasted for long.

I told him that I wouldn't force him to deal with this family secret, but that I couldn't really help him if he was going to let this shame have such power over him. Finally he told me, reluctantly, that his grandfather was significantly involved in the occult—likely one of the reasons his father committed suicide. This family secret had never been dealt with, even though my counsellee's father was a Christian and this young man himself was raised a committed Christian. The reason he had finally decided to see me was because he was struggling with depression, anxiety attacks, and was afraid that he might also take his own life.

The Power of Destructive Secrets

Trying to get this young man to share the family secret was not easy. However, when he dared to open up and trust me, I took steps to expose the lies he believed about himself and his family. He expressed deep anger at his grandfather and father, which I helped him resolve. He opened up about his fear of losing it all, allowing me to deliver him from his demons.

I have heard countless stories of families where the father had uncontrollable rage, or mothers were in constant depression, or one of the siblings was an embarrassment to the family because of their lifestyle choices. Often a fierce sense of pride demands that none of the family secrets ever be shared outside the family circle.

Later on, these family secrets become a "monster" that ends up controlling the whole family. In numerous cases, well-established Christian people never share family secrets that have been hidden for years, for fear that the family would lose their good reputation. Because these individuals have never worked through the shame from their family of origin, they end up bringing shame from their past into their own immediate families.

Interestingly, sometimes the family secrets are not really that horrendous. However, they grow so much larger by remaining buried for years. These shameful secrets can become magnified to mammoth proportions. The emotional system is constantly on guard in case these secrets ever become revealed. The shame issues may not be large, but when they are held in secret they gain energy, strength, and become enormous.

Destructive secrets are like a small snowball at the top of a hill. As the snowball rolls down the hill it gains in size, momentum, and velocity. Likewise, these shame secrets gain energy by hiding. Over time, they get larger and larger and their impact grows.

The Cost of Unresolved Shame

Do we realize the enormous cost to the whole emotional system and its effect on the immune system when we hold this volcanic power of shame within us? Immune system breakdown is significantly impacted by the amount of emotional energy used to sustain shame secrets in our lives. Great amounts of emotional energy are used to keep the "shame door" locked for years. Misplaced emotional energy robs our immune systems of strength to keep us healthy.

Until these shame secrets are worked through in a God-given manner, we are doomed to repeat the same sins (or variations of the same sin) in our immediate families, even though we have vowed otherwise. Destructive secrets are repeated through generation after generation. Repressed feelings of shame lead to the slavery of repeated, destructive behaviour. Exposing our shame secrets, having them forgiven and healed, releases us from a prison of isolation and fear. Until we deal with our shame secrets, we can never truly be free to fulfill God's plan for us.

Finding a Safe Place for Sharing Our Shame Secrets

Deep within each of us lies a fear that if people knew the real me, they would reject me. Or, worse yet, they would even loathe me. If you really knew me, you certainly would not like me. The challenge for us is learning to distinguish between healthy and unhealthy secrets. Shame secrets are totally destructive. Healthy secrets are part of learning to accept our individuality. They are a means to emotional maturity. Therefore, we must find a way to share our destructive secrets without creating more fear and shame.

To deal with our shame secrets, we must find a safe place with God and trusted people. To nullify the power of destructive secrets, we must open up to a safe person whom we can trust implicitly. We must get these shame secrets out of the "closet," confess them, and repent of them (where necessary) to be released from the enemy's power. Remember, at the cross we give up our self-effort to try to "save ourselves." How do we "save ourselves"? We do so by either keeping the door locked or trying to deal with our shame by "doing." When we finally stop crucifying ourselves, we are ready to receive Jesus' sacrifice on the cross as enough.

At the cross we can look at Jesus, hanging there in shame, to receive His forgiveness and cleansing. Then we are freed from carrying our own negative shame and crucifying ourselves repeatedly. When I have personally repented, I have been amazed how wonderful I feel to have that weight removed and to be free from the power of negative shame.

The path we all desire for that freedom is confession, repentance, and obedience. Confession allows us to open the "shame closet door." Repentance removes the "lie" from our thinking to reveal the truth. As

Jesus said in John 8:32 (NIV), "You shall know the truth and the truth will set you free." Obedience allows us to make that truth solidly ours so it becomes a part of our daily behaviour.

Shame versus Freedom

Earlier in the book I used the analogy of a pair of balancing scales. On the one side is shame while on the other side is freedom. We have to decide to which scale we will give more weight. That decision holds far-reaching consequences. If we decide to hold on to our shame secrets, we may never get released from their impact on our lives. If we choose freedom, we must risk dealing with fear within. We also have to risk finding someone safe to share our shame secrets.

Our challenge pits the risk of hanging on to shame against the risk of finding a safe place to unload our shame. In my experience with shame, the desire for freedom outweighed the fear of rejection. By keeping our secrets, we have been trusting ourselves in order to stay in control. We need to pray: "I'm going to trust you, Jesus, to work out this shame for me in a safe and healthy way. Father God, I believe You will protect me and lead me to the freedom I have been seeking."

This decision for freedom delivers major consequences for you from this day. Your decision today may even be as basic as to say: "I will open the door for God to reveal whatever He wants in my life, in His time and in His way." But we must have a greater desire for freedom than we have fear of rejection. We must be willing to release the control of our lives from ourselves to Jesus.

I understand this spiritual battle to be enormous. I have fought this battle myself more than once. Think of yourself as a warrior. It doesn't matter if you are male or female (think about Joan of Arc, the young heroine who fought for the French in the Hundred Years War in the fifteenth century), young or old, new Christian or seasoned Christian. You declare war on the spirit of shame over you, your family, church, or city. You want freedom more than anything else, and you are willing to risk rejection in order to get that freedom.

I know that freedom from shame will not come in a day, but you must declare your intention to keep working for this freedom until you know that you are walking in the freedom of Christ every day. If you are not ready, then as you read this book, do NOT feel condemned. But I would encourage you to honestly tell Father God about your fears. Tell Him you want freedom but you are afraid. Ask Him to help you step over the threshold. He is entirely on your side. He is a "good, good Father" as one song says.

An Exercise for Your Development

Having read Part 5 of the book, now write on a piece of paper or in your notebook one issue in your life in which you want freedom. Then write the name of the person with whom you are willing to share your shame secret. Pray for courage to follow through with what you have written.

PART 6

Learning to Use Positive Shame for Growth

CHAPTER 27

Focusing on Positive Shame

Up to this point in time, I primarily have been focusing on the negative aspects of shame. For most of us the negative side of shame dominates our lives. We focused on eliminating its powerful grip. Despite the fact that shame is dominated by its negative side, shame has a positive aspect. (We briefly introduced positive shame in the beginning of the book.) God wants us to turn negative shame into positive shame. He wants us to learn to use positive shame to enable us to live a healthy lifestyle.

Earlier, I said that negative shame is about hiding; positive shame is about boundaries. A society that is without shame, without standards of right and wrong will produce a people who are dishonourable and indecent. They may feel "liberated," but they are actually enslaved to the shame behaviours in their lives. They believe they have license to do whatever they want, but in so doing they become addicted to obsessive thoughts and compulsive behaviours.

Movie stars openly display their sexuality on television or other media outlets and howl their obscenities, because they believe their right to do so. Politicians lie without conscience. Then they maintain their political offices despite their shameful behaviour and expect to be reelected. Even after their shame is exposed, they write books proudly telling all, so they can make more money from a society hungry to hear gossip.

The expression "Have you no shame" is appropriate as a descriptor of our society today. We are shameful yet proud of it. We are a culture that has hidden so much of our shameful behaviour, yet we are becoming more "shameless" all the time. We have too much negative shame and not enough positive shame. A society without positive shame is in serious trouble, inviting the inevitable judgment of God.

Humility Opens the Door of Shame

For shame to become positive for us, we first must deal with our negative shame. The only way that negative shame can be resolved is through humility. Negative shame is so "shameful" that without humility shame cannot come out of the "locked closet door." Why? Because, as the Bible says, "God gives His grace to the humble" (1 Peter 5:5 NIV). Grace is the empowering presence of God in our lives, which enables us to move from the kingdom of darkness into the kingdom of light. God's grace enables us to live out kingdom principles within a dark world.

Simply put, we need God's grace to enable us to open the "door of negative shame." The power of negative shame must be confronted by the greater power of grace. In Scripture, God will not give His grace to anyone who does not approach God in humility. Pride says, "I've got it all worked out, so I don't need any help." Pride also says, "My solution is to keep all my unresolved sin locked up in the "closet of shame.""

Whenever we decide the best thing we can do is to leave negative shame locked up, we are choosing pride. We think we can solve our shame issues by ourselves without God's grace. But shame is significantly more powerful than we realize. We cannot deal with shame without God's powerful gift of grace.

I have been using the analogy of a "locked door" or "locked closet" to describe what most of us do with our negative shame. Who has the key to this "locked door of shame?" You do. And humility is the key that opens the "door of negative shame" in our lives. Pride is the lock on the door. The only way to unlock the "closet" is with the "key of humility." We must use the "key of humility" or we will not have access to the "closet of shame."

Turning Negative Shame into Positive Shame

Once we open the "door of shame," the Holy Spirit can turn our negative shame into positive shame. When we allow the Holy Spirit to do this for us and in us, we make a paradigm shift. We experience the freedom that Jesus Christ died to give us. When we share with others what the gospel has done to free us, we will draw others, who also want to be set free, to Jesus. We can testify to the truth that God is continually transforming our lives. We can say, "See what He did for me today" (not twenty or thirty or forty years ago).

We are constantly in need of being changed. If the gospel is not relevant for every day and for transforming us every day, we are living in religion. One thing I know: we won't be transformed fully this side of heaven. That means we continually need the Holy Spirit to make changes in us. In order for others to see growth in us, we need to tell our stories of transformation. If we don't have ongoing transformation occurring in our lives, we only can share our stories of twenty (or more) years ago.

Over the years of hearing many speakers at conferences, I know I was impacted most by those speakers who dared to teach the Word of God with authority, but also by sharing their own vulnerability. I always am as interested in seeing how the gospel is working in their lives as I am in how well they spoke or the insights they brought from God's Word.

I have never forgotten years ago when my spiritual father, Duane Harder, came to visit us in Lethbridge. After he got off the plane and I asked him how he was doing, he said, "Well, I left Marva (his wife) in tears at the Kelowna airport because of a conflict we had just before I flew to Lethbridge." I didn't know Duane as well in those days but I was blown away by his honesty and vulnerability. That probably meant more to me than whatever teaching he did that weekend at our church.

I remember hearing Dr. John White, the well-known Christian psychiatrist and author (now deceased), speaking in our city of Lethbridge. His teaching was always impacting, but what stayed in my memory more than his teaching on this occasion was his vulnerability while he spoke. I thought to myself, *I hope one day I have the courage to be so open and honest.* My respect for both these men increased with their willingness to walk humbly before God's people.

God's Transforming Power

If the gospel is as powerful as Romans 1:16 (NIV) tells us, (and it is) then it ought to be transforming us on a daily basis. "I am not ashamed of the gospel, because it is the power of God for the salvation of everyone who believes." I love hearing the stories from those working in other countries as to how the gospel is transforming whole communities. But it also must transform us individually on an ongoing basis or the stories are just stories.

When we find ourselves ashamed of the gospel, it may indicate that we have not truly experienced God's transforming power in our lives. The gospel is the **power** of God to transform every area of our hearts. Period! The issue is not the power of the gospel but our ability to believe it, receive it, and experience it. It **is** the power of God, not it **was** the power of God. God wants it to be a present experience in our lives, not just a past theological understanding.

When we find ourselves ashamed of the gospel, we need to allow the shame to alert us to the unreality of our faith at that moment. That's how negative shame can function as an emotional signal—telling us we need to adjust our unbelief. When we are ashamed of the gospel, we are too concerned with what people think of us. That is called pride. Pride functions as a false protection for when we feel insecure about ourselves.

Will That Be Pride or Humility?

I have heard the Holy Spirit say to me countless times, "Graham, will you humble yourself or remain in your pride?" Humility opens the "door" for me to examine my shame and its cause. Humility wrestles with pride. Which one wins is up to me; I make the choice.

I still vividly remember an incident in our home with our son, Andy. He was probably about twenty years old at the time. Andy had been away at Bible School in Scotland and had returned home for a year or so. We had just finished supper one night when I asked our two younger sons, Nathan and Caleb, to clean up the table and wash the dishes. I didn't want to do it myself, because I wanted to watch the six o'clock news.

I came back into the kitchen at the first commercial break to see how the boys were doing with the dishes. Nothing had been done, and they were both having a good time playing. I spoke angrily to them about getting the dishes done. At that point, Andy came to me and said, "Dad, can I say something to you?" He spoke to me respectfully and graciously. I gulped but said yes. Andy said, "It seems to me you have not been following through with your responsibility as a father."

At that moment, I was trying to decide how to respond to Andy's statement to me. I was aware of the battle within me between pride and humility. I wanted to defend myself (pride), but I knew he was speaking the truth and I should open myself up to his correction (humility). The picture I often have in my mind is an angel on one shoulder telling me to listen to humility and a demon on the other shoulder saying I have a right to my pride.

In the midst of the "wrestling match" in my mind, the Holy Spirit spoke to me, saying, "Choose humility because that's My way." Fortunately, I chose humility on this occasion and I went back to the family room to turn the television off. I came back to the kitchen, worked alongside my two young sons, training them how to load the dishwasher and scrub the pots and pans. Because I felt the shame by being challenged in my selfishness, I easily could have chosen self-protection instead of humility.

The Value of the Shame Signal

When we dare to share vulnerably, people see the power of the gospel working in our lives. Shame wants to shut things down to hide our sins and mistakes. What people want to see in us is how we handle negative shame. When we find ourselves being ashamed of doing something evil or wrong, shame is signaling us to deal with something. When we respond as the Spirit directs, positive shame is helping us set proper boundaries for doing right.

In this way, shame works in a positive way to bring repentance into our lives with a desire for righteousness. Shame's power now works for us and not against us. We now are ashamed of doing wrong (positive) and ashamed of having anyone seeing us behaving in wrong ways (again, positive shame).

Here are three places in Scripture that illustrate the way shame can work in a positive way for us:

Jeremiah 31:18–20 (NIV)

18 "I have surely heard Ephraim's moaning:
'You disciplined me like an unruly calf,
and I have been disciplined.
Restore me, and I will return,
because you are the Lord my God.
19 After I strayed,

I repented;
after I came to understand,
I beat my breast.
I was ashamed and humiliated
because I bore the disgrace of my youth.'
20 Is not Ephraim my dear son,
the child in whom I delight?
Though I often speak against him,
I still remember him.
Therefore my heart yearns for him;
I have great compassion for him,"
declares the Lord.

What Jeremiah says here is that Israel experienced shame because of her captivity in Babylon. It was working positively for her because it led her to repentance. Jeremiah wanted the people to see that God still loved them, despite allowing them to be punished by being taken into captivity in a foreign land. He was telling them how much God yearned for them to respond to the shame they felt in their captivity, returning to Him to experience God's way out of this captivity. Shame in that sense was working positively for the Jewish people.

Positive Shame Helps Us Do What Is Right

Ezra 8:21–23 (NIV)

21 There, by the Ahava Canal, I proclaimed a fast, so that we might humble ourselves before our God and ask him for a safe journey for us and our children, with all our possessions.

22 I was ashamed to ask the king for soldiers and horsemen to protect us from enemies on the road, because we had told the king, "The gracious hand of our God is on everyone who looks to him, but his great anger is against all who forsake him."

23 So we fasted and petitioned our God about this, and he answered our prayer.

Ezra is telling us that he boasted about God's hand of protection and provision to the king and now he is too ashamed to ask the king for soldiers to go with them for protection. This is positive shame in action because it pressed the Jews into trusting God even though they were naturally afraid and wanted the additional protection of the soldiers. Positive shame caused them to walk in faith rather than in fear. As a result, when they fasted and prayed to God, He answered their prayer. Positive shame can move us to trust God in spite of our fears.

2 Thessalonians 3:14–15 (NIV)

14 "If anyone does not obey our instruction in this letter, take special note of him. Do not associate with him, in order that he may feel ashamed.

15 Yet do not regard him as an enemy, but warn him as a brother."

We need to be careful how we use shame because it can condemn and alienate us from people. But Paul is telling the Thessalonian church that by not associating with a Christian brother, one who is not obeying Paul's instructions, a feeling of shame will come on him. This is positive shame that is used to draw this disobedient Christian back into doing right. He also tells the Thessalonian Christians not to use shame to make this brother feel like an enemy but to use it to motivate him to repent of his wrong behaviour. This is shame used in a right way and, therefore, positive shame.

Using Shame for Positive Changes

This is one of the challenges for Christians today. How can we use shame in our churches to bring positive change and without condemnation? Typically people get offended when confronted and then move to another church. Only the enemy wins in that case, no repentance and no behaviour changes for the individual. For positive shame to work in our churches today, we need to make the fellowship of the church family so precious that when people are challenged they do not want to leave but want to work to resolve issues.

The cross of Christ brings an exchange of values in shame. Before we came to the cross, shame was negative and functioned as our enemy. When we bring our negative shame to the cross for forgiveness, we can use its transformational power as a motivator for doing the will of God. We don't want to stand before Jesus on the Judgment Day and be ashamed—a personal motivation for me. I am motivated to do what is right because I want to hear Jesus say, "Well done, good and faithful servant."

Mark 8:38 (NIV) reminds us: "If anyone is ashamed of me and my words in this adulterous and sinful generation, the Son of Man will be ashamed of him when he comes in his Father's glory with the holy angels."

Being ashamed of God is not good at all. It can lead us to deny him, whereupon Jesus says He will deny us. Humility is the only means by which we can examine our denial of Jesus to turn things around. Humility turns negative shame into positive shame. And positive shame is what God uses to keep us walking in purity, wholesomeness, righteousness, and holiness.

This is also how God wants to use positive shame to help us walk in sexual purity in an age in which morality is quickly discarded.

CHAPTER 28

SHAME AND SEXUALITY

Probably the most significant area where shame has control over our lives is sexuality. Numerous illustrations appear in Scripture. Rahab and Salmon in the Old Testament and Joseph and Mary in the New Testament are positive examples. Samson, Judah, David and Bathsheba (God redeemed these situations but at a price) are negative examples. The enemy is working overtime in this area of sexuality because he knows he can keep God's people from reaching spiritual maturity if he keeps them dealing with sexual impurity.

When God created man and woman in the Garden they were naked. That means that God blessed the freedom of their nakedness. Before the advent of sin, they did not experience any shame in that natural state because they didn't need shame as an emotional signal to warn them of any danger. They did not experience any kind of shame in their nakedness because there was nothing to cause shame. However, once they disobeyed God, ate the forbidden fruit, and stepped outside of the boundaries that God had placed for them, Adam and Eve brought guilt and shame into their lives.

Interestingly, God only gave them one boundary, which was not to eat of the forbidden fruit of the Tree of the Knowledge of Good and Evil. But that one boundary was enough for them to be tested, and unfortunately for all of us they failed that test. Satan deceived Eve into believing that God was holding out on her. Adam, however, chose Eve over God, because he didn't want to lose this beautiful creature that God had given him. When they listened to the serpent and decided they wanted to "run their own show," they doubted God's love and care for them. When Satan questioned God's love, they falsely believed that God was holding out.

Guilt and Shame as Positive Emotional Signals

When they disobeyed God's specific command, they stepped outside of God's protective boundary. At that point, God introduced shame and guilt into their emotional repertoire. Although shame and guilt were the consequence of sin, they also served, in a positive sense, as emotional signals to prevent them from ongoing sin. God took the mess that Adam and Eve created and provided protection for them from further sin by alerting them to sin through guilt and shame.

Without the boundaries of positive shame, we can return to the state of rebellion where "everyone did as he saw fit" (Judges 21:25 NIV)). After Joshua died, the Israelites failed to raise up other godly leaders. For the period of the "judges," they constantly did whatever was right in their own eyes. So they became a shameless society. We are seeing the same result in our North American culture today. To a large extent, we have lost the capacity to determine what is right and what is wrong.

As a shameless society, we are unable to distinguish between modesty and brashness. We can't tell the difference between sexual restraint and sexual exploitation. So many children are growing up in homes today where there are no boundaries regarding sexuality. As these children get into their teen years, they follow whatever sexual urges come. As a result, sexual exploitation is rampant. We are constantly hearing stories in the news media about one mess after another.

The only way our society can develop people of integrity, nobility, discretion, and honour is allowing positive shame to set boundaries for what is right and wrong with regard to sexuality. God as our Creator is the One who sets the boundaries for what is wholesome, healthy, and right in regard to sexual expression. Because we leave God out of our lives and our society, we do "whatever feels good." God has put limitations in place, just like He did in the garden, so we will avoid using one another. He is also giving us these boundaries so we can honour one another by respecting each other's privacy.

Positive Shame Helps Control Sexual Urges

God established in His Word that we don't have the right to walk into someone's home and take whatever we want. This law is one of the Ten Commandments (Thou shalt not steal). Just because we like something and have the urge to take does not mean we have the right. The area of sexuality is the same. Even though we are attracted to the opposite sex, we do not have the right to use them for our own desires. A society that has learned to accept sexual boundaries is a safe society. A society that believes it has the right to do whatever it wants to another person, regarding sex, is a chaotic society. Positive shame helps set up healthy boundaries that agree with the way God designed a healthy society to function.

I counselled a couple who initially came to see me because of communication issues and financial disagreements. They were fighting a great deal over a number of issues, but money was a major area of conflict. As I was looking for the root of their conflict, I asked the question (by the Holy Spirit), "Were you sexually involved before you married?" I immediately saw shame on her face and he wouldn't look at me. I told them I wanted to know how they came into their marriage, because for me it is a major clue as to what kind of a foundation they set for their marriage.

They told me, after drinking heavily one night, in a state of drunkenness, they had sexual intercourse. But they assured me it only happened once. Three years after that event, they got married. But as I watched their nonverbals, particularly hers, I knew they were not telling me the whole truth. I decided to see them separately to take their histories, which is something I sometimes do.

Current major conflicts in marriage often result from what was brought into the marriage by both spouses. I met with the husband first to see if I could determine what attitudes and values he had carried into the marriage. Then I began meeting with the wife to see what she would tell me. As I was exploring her perspective of their sexual relationship, I noticed a lot of shame. As we talked about it, I told her that I sensed that this area of sexuality was shameful for her.

Listening to her, I realized that her husband was sexually abusing her even though they were married. He had been to some nightclubs with lewd sexual acts and he came home with the desire to practice this perversity on his wife. Her sexual values were being violated again and again. I told her I suspected that a lot more happened in their sexual relationship before they got married than what they had first disclosed. "Yes," she confessed. They did have intercourse once but they had regular oral sex for three years before they married. Because they didn't actually have vaginal intercourse, they told me that they had not had sexual relations after that one incident.

Positive Shame Brings Freedom

God sets a boundary for sexual relations and that boundary is marriage. Sexual relations before marriage is called fornication (a word we don't use much any more). A married person having sex with someone other than his or her spouse is called adultery. God doesn't set those boundaries to restrict us from pleasure but to protect us from destructive relationships. Because Father God created us, He knows what works and doesn't in the area of sexuality.

God gives us these boundaries so that in marriage we are able to fully enjoy the sexual pleasure God intended for marriage. I realize that many people reading this book will have stepped outside those boundaries. Again, let me say that my purpose in this writing is not to bring condemnation on you and create more shame for you, but to help you correct what needs to be corrected so you can live joyfully in the boundaries of God. He wants to take the negative experiences from our past and show us where we have stepped over the boundary lines so we can repent. God's goal is to redeem us from our past sins. We still have this idea that time heals past issues—not so. Time just buries them for a period of years, only to have the shame surface in some other form. Because Father God loves us so much, He doesn't want us to live in negative shame for the rest of our lives.

When we step outside God's boundaries, we don't function in more freedom but less freedom. When Sherry and I do pre-marriage counselling with young couples, we ask them if they have engaged in sexual relations. We are not trying to shame them, but bring to attention those things in the past that will keep them from starting their marriage on a wrong foundation. If these areas are not confessed, repented of, and choices made to stay within God's boundaries, then possibly ten or fifteen years after we will be dealing with a variety of relational issues, including sexual problems.

Reaping What We Sow

Sometimes unresolved secret sexual sins may appear to have no impact in one's marriage. But consequences always follow unresolved guilt in our lives. Galatians 6:7–8 (NIV) reminds us, "Do not be deceived. God cannot be mocked. A man reaps what he sows. The one who sows to please his sinful nature, from that nature will reap destruction; the one who sows to please the Spirit will reap eternal life." Why does the Holy Spirit use the phrase, "Do not be deceived"? Because so many of us are deceived! We may not see or feel guilt for a time and if we do, we may think we don't have to deal with our unresolved guilt and shame.

God has given us the Bible, the Holy Spirit, godly parents (some of us), and godly spouses to help us walk within the boundaries that He has set for our good. He wants us to function in guilt-free sexual relationships.

Sexuality is not just for married people. Single people are sexual beings as well. Healthy sexuality has to do with all of us enjoying the liberty of our maleness or our femaleness. Sexuality is not merely referring to sexual intercourse, nor about being in bed with someone. It means accepting and enjoying our maleness or femaleness. All the parts of our bodies are meant to be holy. God created our bodies and our sexual organs to be used as instruments of righteousness (Romans 6:11–14). Sexuality means enjoying the freedom of our maleness and femaleness, which God gave us when we were formed in our mother's wombs.

The Joy of Sexual Purity

A woman's body and her sexuality is a gift from God to be kept pure until the day she marries and can give herself fully to her husband as a gift. The same is true for men. When Father God gave Sherry to me as my wife, He was giving me His daughter. In the same way that I honoured Sherry's earthly father, Alvin Dirks, by how I treat his daughter, I also want to honour her heavenly Father by how I love and cherish her. One day when I stand and give an account to Jesus for my words and my deeds (Matthew 12:36; Romans 14:11–12; Hebrews 4:13), I don't want to stand before Him and be ashamed.

When we fail to function in sexual wholeness, significant consequences affect our lives. Romans 1 is a commentary of what happens when we live outside the boundaries of godly sexuality. Romans 1:18–19 (NIV) says: "The wrath of God is being revealed from heaven against all the godlessness and wickedness of men who suppress the truth by their wickedness, since what may be known about God is plain to them because God has made it plain to them."

Romans 1:26–27 (NIV) also reminds us: "Because of this God gave them over to shameful lusts. Even their women exchanged natural relations for unnatural ones. In the same way the men also abandoned natural relations with women and were inflamed with lust for one another. Men committed indecent acts with other men and received in themselves the due penalty for their perversion."

Today, taking a stand against homosexuality is not at all popular. The gay community has turned the tables on what the Bible teaches and has made Christians and many others with high moral standards the "bad guys" for daring to challenge this sexual perversion. I didn't make the above statements. God did. But I can say I fully agree with God's Word, as unpopular as it may be today. I do not feel negative toward the homosexual community. God loves them (and asks Christians to love them too) as much as He loves the Christian community, but whatever God calls sin is sin.

The Boundaries of Protection

Notice that the passage in Romans 1 says that God gave them over to their shameful lusts. What this verse means is that God removed the boundaries of protection from them when they continued to live in disobedience to God's Word. So God is saying, in essence, if you don't want to stay within His boundaries, He will remove His protection and you will experience the penalty that comes from living in a shameless society.

If we choose to live within the boundaries that God sets, negative shame is unnecessary. We are free to enjoy this gift of intimacy, just as Adam and Eve were free to enjoy their nakedness in the Garden of Eden before they sinned against God. When we step outside those boundaries, we experience guilt as a signal. If we ignore the guilt signal and don't repent when we have wronged God, shame covers the guilt and we have lost the value of the guilt signal to correct our behaviour. Because we are ashamed of our shame, we ignore the guilt signal. But not responding to the guilt signal is to our detriment.

When we carry negative shame in our sexual lives, we are not free to fully enjoy all the intimacy that God intended for sexual expression. The answer to this dilemma is to pay attention to the guilt signal, confess whatever we need to confess, repent of believing the lie that has led us into this sin in the first place, and obey what we now know to be true and right.

Living within God's boundaries also means we become freer to enjoy our maleness and our femaleness. Men can be men with no need to wish they were females, and females can fully enjoy their femaleness without desiring to be men. Men don't have to dominate women because they are afraid of them, and women don't have to control men because they are afraid of them.

All Locked Up

The weight of unresolved shame leaves people locked up inside. When this occurs in marriage, both men and women often look outside of their marriages for relationships that will satisfy them. They do this because of the lie they believe about themselves. The lie tells them that they can find this elusive freedom they are looking for with another woman or man. On the other hand, when one is enjoying the best of intimacy with one's marriage partner, why would he or she look elsewhere for another partner?

If this discussion touches uncomfortable emotions in you or raises thoughts in your mind about your situation, then I urge you to seek some help from a trustworthy counsellor. If you want to live in freedom, you must deal with your guilt or shame. If you feel too ashamed to deal with your shame, where do you suppose that lie is coming from? The enemy of our souls will do anything to keep this lie hidden in shame to prevent us from correcting this sin.

Proverbs 28:13 (NIV) reminds us that "he who conceals his sins does not prosper, but whoever confesses and renounces them finds mercy." When we confess and renounce our sin, God's mercy enables us to see what is right and in that, we begin to prosper. Our fear is that if we have to confess we have sinned or missed the mark, we will be condemned for our failure—but that is not true. God knows none of us can live perfectly. That's why, in His mercy, He gives us the gift of confession so we can unload our sin and get rid of its effect in our lives.

God wants to turn our sexual failures and sins (through confession) into growth and development. This would be a good time to put the book down and ask the Holy Spirit to show you anything He has been speaking to you concerning what you have just read. As the saying goes, "Strike while the iron is hot." Now is the right time to reflect on what God might be speaking to you in this area of sexuality and shame.

Thank you, Father, for this gift of sexuality. Thank you that You made each of us male or female. You have declared sexuality good and You bless it. Thank you that you do not condemn us for our sexual failures but You desire to show us mercy whenever we bring our confession to You. Father, you are making us hungry for intimacy with You and with our family members. You long to see this area of our lives redeemed and brought back into wholeness. You desire to see intimacy in our marriages that reflects the intimacy we see between You, Father, and Your beloved Son. As we are listening to your Spirit, we ask You to speak into our spirits with Your love and acceptance.

CHAPTER 29

Using Positive
Shame for Growth

Using positive shame for our growth means learning where God's boundaries are and learning to live in the freedom of those boundaries. People often feel that a discussion about boundaries is restrictive. A train may not seem free because it is restricted to running on the tracks, but the tracks are what allows the train to function in what it is created to be. The train needs the tracks to be useful. Truly the tracks restrict the train, yet the tracks also give the train freedom to carry its cargo efficiently. Without tracks the train is useless.

We were created to be free people, just as Adam and Eve were created to be free in the Garden before sin. The boundaries of the Garden were intended to give them freedom. God set "tracks" for them to run on that would give them maximum joy and pleasure. We are the same. If, in our rebellion or pride, we tell God we'd rather function without His "tracks," He will allow us to derail so we learn that the "tracks" are there for our good. If we want to find fulfillment in our lives, we need to ask God to show us the "tracks" He has designed for us.

I want to share four areas where the "restriction" (so called) of positive shame can be utilized for our growth and development.

Positive Shame Can Bring People to God

1 Corinthians 1:26–30 (NIV): "Brothers think of what you were when you were called. Not many of you were wise by human standards, not many were influential, not many were of noble birth, but God chose the foolish things of the world to shame the wise. God chose the weak things of the world to shame the strong. He chose the lowly things of this world, the despised things, the things that are not to nullify the things that are so no one may boast before him. It is because of him that you are in Christ Jesus who has become for us wisdom from God, that is our righteousness, holiness and redemption."

The greatest sin for mankind is his independence from God and the rebellion that resulted. Since Adam made his choice in the Garden, we have inherited this same tendency to run on our own "tracks." The sin of pride or independence started with Satan in heaven; he brought it to earth. He deceived Adam and Eve into thinking they were better off controlling their own lives. In 1 Corinthians 1, Paul tells us that God is reversing this independence we inherited from the Garden. He is going to use the so-called foolish things of the world to bring to us an awareness of how much we need God in our lives.

Finding out that none of us can live without God is freeing. Satan deceived us into thinking that we can get along quite well without Him. Because of rebellion, Adam and Eve realize they needed a "covering," which God provided. When they hid in shame, they realized they still needed God in their lives. Before long, we too realize we mess up badly without Him.

When I was working at Lethbridge College, I was asked by a colleague to go with him to another college in Alberta to do an evaluation of their student services area. We spent four days working together to assess the functionality of all the services at this other college, services like counselling, financial aid, registration, et cetera. During lunches and suppers together, we talked quite personally.

He asked me about my family, my background, where I was born and raised. I shared my Christian upbringing and theological training. He knew I was a pastor so I shared some of my philosophy of life. I asked him, in return, about his upbringing and his family. He told me he was raised in the Catholic Church and he shared some of his views about Christianity. I have to say this about my colleague: he was one of the best men I ever worked with. He was a quality family man, an excellent counsellor for our department, and a man of integrity. He was well liked by our department, and the others also felt the same way about him as I did.

At one point, I asked him why, in his Catholic faith, he never really pursued God. Did he see any need to commit his life to follow Jesus Christ? His answer to me was this: "I have lived a good life and I don't really see that I need God in my life." He had no real awareness of sin in his life. Without an awareness of sin in our lives, we think we really don't need God. We need an awareness of sin to show us that we need God more than we know. We can't live life fully without God.

When God wants to bring punishment on people, He removes their shame covering. He leaves them shameless. Negative shame allows us to see who we really are without God. Positive shame brings us awareness that we need God in our lives. When we don't live within the "restrictions" or boundaries of shame, we are imprisoned by our so-called "freedom." We think we are living in the freedom of our own choices, but we soon discover the consequences for running our own show.

People are free only within the God-given boundaries that He established. When we live in this "freedom," it is powerfully attractive to many people in the world who recognize that their shameful lifestyles are not really freedom at all. Christians who have learned to live in the boundaries that God sets have such joy in this freedom that it is genuinely attractive to a world looking for real joy. Within the boundaries of God are "righteousness, peace and joy in the Holy Spirit" (Romans 14:17 NIV).

Positive Shame Acts as a Warning Signal

1 Corinthians 15:33–34 (NIV): "Do not be misled. Bad company corrupts good character. Come back to your senses as you ought and stop sinning. For there are some who are ignorant of God. I say this to your shame."

Paul is not trying to shame the Corinthian Christians in a negative sense. He is using shame in a positive way to alert them to their sinful lifestyle so they will stop destroying their lives. He was warning them, through positive shame, that hanging around with bad company corrupts their character. Positive shame can act as a warning signal that tells us we are living outside the boundaries of God.

2 Thessalonians 3:14 (NIV): "If anyone does not obey our instructions in this letter take special note of him and do not associate with

him in order that he may feel ashamed." Positive shame acts as a signal to alert Christians that their sinful lifestyle is counterproductive to a life of joy and freedom. To turn negative shame into positive shame, we must pay attention to what the shame signal is saying. Shame, as an emotional signal, is designed to warn us that we are going off God's "track" of righteous living.

The signal that God has given us for "daily" sins is guilt. But when guilt is continuously ignored, it turns into unconscious shame. So the Holy Spirit will also use shame as a signal that we have stepped outside the boundaries of God. When we notice we feel ashamed about something in our behaviour or attitudes, it is God signaling us that we need to examine why we are feeling ashamed. When we do confess our sin because of the shame signal, negative shame is now turned into positive shame.

Using Shame to Keep Holy

Of course Satan doesn't want us paying attention to the shame signal, so he will use our shame to accuse us. When we buy into his accusations, then we naturally bury the shame signal, because we don't like to feel accused. When we sense the shame signal, we have to remind ourselves not to listen to the accusation of the enemy. The truth from God's perspective is that when we sin He gives mercy, forgiveness, and cleansing.

In this sense, the shame signal operates much like the guilt signal, even though shame and guilt are too different emotions. For example, you can watch something unwholesome on television or on the internet and feel ashamed for what you are seeing. This is the Holy Spirit signaling you that you ought not to be feeding your soul with garbage. You can be standing on a street corner, in a shopping mall, or in an airport and realize, through the shame signal, that you are observing what you shouldn't.

God alerts us to this shame signal so we can correct it. When we ignore the shame signal or listen to the condemnation of the enemy, we lose the value of positive shame trying to help us. If, on the other hand, we pay attention to the signal and respond positively to it, then our negative shame is turned into positive shame. The more we positively respond to shame, the more conscious we are of the value of shame for our growth and development.

I am aware as I write this that God has trained me to pay attention to the shame signal. Obviously, like you, I may not always pay attention to it the first time. But increasingly I am aware of how shame can work for me instead of against me. When we realize that we can't out-sin God's mercy and grace, we become hopeful for a way out of perpetual sin. Positive shame serves as a warning signal to keep us in the boundaries of God and keep us safe from the temptations and manipulations of the enemy.

Positive Shame Challenges Wrong Thinking

1 Corinthians 6:1–6 (NIV): "If any of you has a dispute with another dare you take it before the ungodly for judgment instead of before the saints. Do you not know that the saints will judge the world? If you are to judge the world are you not competent to judge trivial cases? Do you not know we will judge angels? How much more the things of this life. Therefore, if you have disputes about such matters appoint as judges

even men of little account in the church. I say this to shame you. But instead one brother goes to law against another brother. And this in front of the unbelievers."

Paul is challenging the carnal Corinthian church for its immaturity in dealing with their conflicts. He uses shame to bring conviction to faulty thinking. The Corinthians seem to have forgotten that they have the power of the Holy Spirit in them to help them settle disputes within the church community. They don't need to take conflicts to secular society to deal with matters. More wisdom is available in the church than in the world, but we must access that wisdom through the Holy Spirit. We need to hear this message loud and clear in the church today.

Do you remember when, as a child, you experienced instances of shame? You knew you were caught doing something wrong and you could feel the shame in your emotions (and sometimes in your body). At that point, you made a decision about what to do with the shame you were feeling.

I well remember a time when I was caught telling a lie to my parents. When they confronted me with the lie, I remember the great shame I felt at that moment. But that shameful experience stopped me from heading into a direction in which I would lie all the time. God used my shame to reroute my negative thinking that lying would give me an advantage to get ahead in life. This shame experience was certainly not nice, but it was powerful in helping me change where I was heading.

This is what the Holy Spirit is saying to the Corinthian Christians in this section of Scripture. He is telling them to pay attention to the shame signal so that they won't continue to take their disputes from the church to secular courts for resolution. Shame, functioning in a positive sense, can correct serious breaches in a person's or a church's life. When leaders cover up shame in the church, they create irreparable damage to the life of the fellowship. Sometimes a church needs to come to the place where it experiences its own shame. Hopefully that will lead to a place of repentance.

Positive shame is meant to be a powerful signal to keep us from violating principles of God's Word. For the church to mature and grow, it must function within the boundaries of God's Word and God's will. Outside the boundaries of God's laws lies real danger. We may not see it but God does; He will use shame to alert us to that danger.

Just as parents understand dangers that their children do not see, so God understands dangers that His children do not see. Because parents see more than their children, they keep their children from crossing dangerous boundaries. Ignoring the shame signal can take people into directions that either ruin their lives or lead them astray for many years.

Positive Shame Motivates
Truth and Responsibility

2 Timothy 2:14–15 (NIV): "Keep reminding them of these things. Warn them before God against quarrelling about words that are of no value and only ruins those who listen. Do your best to present yourself to God as one approved, a workman who does not need to be ashamed, who correctly handles the word of truth."

Here we see that Paul is encouraging Timothy always to use the Word of God in such a way to avoid manipulation. God does not want us using the enemy's strategy to accomplish His purposes. Manipulating is never acceptable in the Kingdom of Light, because manipulation is a form of witchcraft in which the kingdom of darkness specializes.

Over the years some church leaders made plans to build new facilities but didn't wait on the Lord for His timing. They put pressure on their people to sacrifice financially so they could meet their self-imposed timelines. Personal sacrifice is not wrong. However, the Holy Spirit must be the one convincing the church family to give from their hearts. The leadership can certainly share what they believe to be God's plan and timing, but they must never manipulate people to give to satisfy their goals. Let God move His people to give.

Handling the Word of God with Integrity

Positive shame teaches us to be responsible fully with the truth of God's Word. We don't ever want to be ashamed of how we handle it. I believe I have the fear of the Lord within me for how I teach the Scriptures. I have been corrected many times by men of God I have walked under. I also have been corrected by my wife and challenged by my own children. Even the churches I serve have not been afraid to challenge me.

When I teach seminars and workshops, I give feedback sheets to the audience to allow them to correct or challenge what I have been teaching. I want to learn from my audience, whether or not what I have said offended them or I was Biblically correct. I always want to be teachable in how I am presenting the Word of God. Although I may have differences with others on various facets of interpreting the Scriptures, I do not want to be guilty of manipulating God's Word.

I don't want to stand before Jesus one day and have Him correct me for how I manipulated His truth for my advantage. Positive shame is what enables me to hear from others if I have manipulated God's Word for my advantage. Shame acts as a boundary to teach us how to handle the Bible in a right way. Positive shame can also help us handle the truth we teach our families. It can alert and challenge us to walk with truth in our workplaces, communities, and ministry areas.

CHAPTER 30

Turning Shame into Victory for Us

For most of us shame has never been a subject for discussion, nor have we had much interest in it. I was in the same situation myself for years. As a psychologist I was generally aware of the concept of shame, but I could not give you a proper definition of the word. As we come to the conclusion of this book, I want to share some Scripture passages that will help us see how positive shame can aid us to achieve a much greater level of victory in our daily lives.

Faith Is Essential for Shame to Help Us Win the Battle

Romans 10:10–11 (NIV): "For it is with your heart that you believe and are justified. It is with your mouth that you are justified and saved. As the Scripture says, 'Everyone who trusts in him will never be put to shame.'" This passage of Scripture is repeated four times in the Bible (Isaiah 28:16; Romans 9:33; Romans 10:11 and 1 Peter 2:6).

When something repeats in the Bible, it is for emphasis. Like putting something in "bold" letters, we are being directed to see the importance of these words. This passage in Romans is a truth in Scripture that needs attention because it is significant for our growth and development.

In the Garden of Eden Adam and Eve chose to trust themselves, as opposed to God (because they believed Satan's lie). They not only fell into sin and rebellion, but they also were covered with guilt and shame. However, when we respond to God's truth as He desires, our belief in God's Word will give us victory over what the enemy has attempted to use against us. The key issue for us is what we believe. Do we believe the truth or the lie? Peter has a sermon he wants us to hear in the book he wrote. (1 Peter 2:4–12 NIV)

4 "As you come to him, the living Stone—rejected by men but chosen by God and precious to him—

5 you also, like living stones, are being built into a spiritual house to be a holy priesthood, offering spiritual sacrifices acceptable to God through Jesus Christ. 6 For in Scripture it says:

"See, I lay a stone in Zion,
a chosen and precious cornerstone,
and the one who trusts in him
will never be put to shame."

7 Now to you who believe, this stone is precious. But to those who do not believe,

"The stone the builders rejected

has become the capstone,"

8   and,

"A stone that causes men to stumble
and a rock that makes them fall."

They stumble because they disobey the message—
which is also what they were destined for.

9   But you are a chosen people, a royal priesthood, a holy
nation, a people belonging to God, that you may declare
the praises of him who called you out of darkness into his
wonderful light.

10 Once you were not a people, but now you are the people of
God; once you had not received mercy, but now you have
received mercy.

11 Dear friends, I urge you, as aliens and strangers in the
world, to abstain from sinful desires, which war against
your soul.

12 Live such good lives among the pagans that, though they
accuse you of doing wrong, they may see your good deeds
and glorify God on the day he visits us."

The Paradox of Living within Boundaries

If we are truly trusting in God, then we will never be put to shame.
That's quite a statement—which is an absolute promise that God always
will keep. However, the opposite is just as true. When we don't believe
in Jesus, He becomes an offense to us.

When we are living in a genuine trust in God, we don't ever have
anything of which to be ashamed. Think about that! When we live

inside the "shame" boundaries that God has established for us, we trust that God knows what He is doing inside those boundaries; we will live a victorious life with nothing of which to be ashamed. We will live in the victory that Jesus promised us.

Although sounding like a paradox, freedom is found by choosing to live within restraint. To us, freedom means we can do whatever we want. But that is license, not freedom. The Bible defines freedom as living within the boundaries that God has put in place, recognizing that God knows what He is doing. Therefore, the only way to freedom is through faith. Let me say it again, **we trust God that He knows what He is doing!**

I believe the single largest issue in the Christian life is trusting God. I know that to be the biggest challenge in my life. I am always working on trusting God to a greater degree. I know I trust myself a lot more than I trust God (to my shame). To the degree I am able to trust God, I will see expansion and growth in my Christian life.

God sets up boundaries for us, but we think we have a better idea of what those boundaries should be. We look at those boundaries and say to ourselves, "That's too restrictive." However, I have noticed that where I have stayed within God's boundaries, I have found more freedom and joy than setting my own boundaries. I find more of His grace, His delight, His mercy, and His love. Joy is found inside the boundaries that God has placed in my life. The issue for us is trusting that God is right all the time.

Learning to Trust God with My Family

In our family, years after we had three children, we felt God asked us if we had considered His heart for our family in terms of more children. We began to wonder if He was asking us if we would be willing to have more children. From my perspective, I thought our plate was full with the three we had, plus all my other involvement. I did not think I could manage any more. I told the Lord I was doing just fine with three children whom I loved very much. For two years I was challenged with this question.

Like Jacob at Peniel, I eventually lost that wrestling match with the Almighty. And I am so thankful that I did or we would not have had Nathan, Stephen, and Caleb. In 1990, Nathan was born; in 1991, Stephen Graham was stillborn. Although I struggled immensely with God taking our son to heaven, nevertheless I am grateful today for all the lessons I learned through that process. Two years to the day that Stephen died, Caleb was delivered alive and well in 1993.

Inside the boundary of obeying God and having more children, I struggled in my soul. I did not understand God's ways and God's boundaries. I had a major struggle with trusting God after Stephen was stillborn. (I know I am not the only one who wrestles with trusting God.) I asked the question of God, "If these are Your boundaries, why am I feeling so frustrated inside Your 'good' boundaries? I don't feel safe." Ah yes, but there is more to the story than I have yet shared. Allow me to finish the rest of the story about our obedience to God and His good boundaries.

Our son Caleb was born with a knot in his umbilical cord. Because Sherry's womb had been so stretched due to complications in the previous pregnancy with Stephen, plus an overabundance of amniotic fluid, Caleb had plenty of room to "swim." At some point in Sherry's pregnancy, he managed to pass through a loop in his umbilical cord and put a knot in it. When he was coming through the birth canal, he pulled on his umbilical cord.

Our doctor, Gene Boehme, called me over to look at the placenta after Caleb was delivered. He said to me, "Look how green this placenta is. It should be red. He has clearly been stressed in the womb the last while. Caleb is a miracle baby. He could have easily died in utero because his oxygen supply was increasingly being cut off by the knot." All through Sherry's pregnancy with Caleb, we both prayed fervently for God's protection over our baby because of what had happened to Stephen. How thankful we are for God's protection and mercy in our lives.

Living from Faith to Faith

Remember Romans 1:16 (NIV)? "I am not ashamed of the gospel, because it is the power of God for the salvation of everyone who believes: first for the Jew, then for the Gentile."

The whole point of the gospel, which is such good news, is saying I trust you God with my life. I believe Your Word is truth and I am staking my life and my eternity on believing that the Bible is telling the truth. I am choosing to believe "You are the way, the **truth**, and the life" even when it costs me in this life. It may cost us in our lifestyles and in our finances. We may have to go through pain, confusion, and even loss of life. But somehow we come to the conclusion that despite it all, God is good and He is trustworthy.

We do not live by faith only to enter the Kingdom of God. We live by faith in our daily lives. We are, as Romans 1:17 says, living from faith to faith. We are trusting God again and again and again. About the time I think I have become secure in trusting God in my life, guess what? God opens up another area of my life to develop further faith in Him. Why? Because God wants me to learn to trust Him in every sphere of my life.

Faith is this ability to look into the eyes of Jesus and know that He can be trusted in every test of life. Faith is also the means by which I can look into Jesus' eyes and not have any negative shame. We all know the childhood experience of doing something wrong and not being able to look our parents in the eye because of our shame. This joy is living in positive shame: we have accepted the boundaries of God and fully enjoy our life within His boundaries. This place is the ultimate place of freedom. We are free to be whom God has made us to be.

Living in Positive Shame through Following Jesus' Example

Hebrews 12:1–3 (NIV): "Therefore since we are surrounded by such a great cloud of witnesses, let us throw off everything that hinders and the sin that so easily entangles, and let us run with perseverance the race marked out for us. Let us fix our eyes on Jesus, the author and perfecter of our faith, who for the joy set before him endured the cross, scorning its shame, and sat down at the right hand of the throne of God. Consider him who endured such opposition from sinful men, so you will not grow weary and lose heart."

Jesus was able to look at the shame of the cross and scorn its destructive power. He chose the difficult route of the cross, obeying

His Father so we could be set free. You see, even Jesus had to trust His Father in the Garden of Gethsemene. Jesus asked His Father if there was another way. I don't believe His concern was just the horror of what He knew was coming in the physical suffering on the cross. I believe Jesus' "fear" was the horror of being separated from His Father for the first time in all eternity because He carried our sin.

He asked His Father for any other way to accomplish God's plan of salvation. His Father said, "No, there is no other way." Jesus said, "Not my will but Yours be done." Just like us, Jesus was in a wrestling match. But He chose to live (and die) within the boundaries of God. The fear for Jesus was the separation from His Father because of carrying our sin. The internal pressure on Jesus was so great that the capillaries in His body burst and He was "sweating" blood.

Jesus Lived within Boundaries

Jesus was willing to live within His Father's boundaries. He was not ashamed to do what God asked Him even though most people of His day would have thought Jesus was dying for His own mistakes and sins. To most people looking on, it looked like Jesus finished His life in defeat. Of course, this journey started with Jesus spending nine months in the womb of His mother whom He created. Not only did Jesus, the Son of God, have this human body for thirty-three years, but also He has humbled Himself to have this body (although glorified) for all of eternity.

Amazing! Jesus walks in the "shame" of His humanness for all eternity (not that Jesus lives in any human shame, in the sense of what we walk in). When Jesus came back in His resurrected body, He said to

Thomas. "Here, put your finger in the holes in my hands, put your fist in my side." His resurrected body still carried the wounds of the cross. He will bear those scars for all eternity and will not be ashamed of them.

The example Jesus sets for us is that He is not ashamed to live within the boundaries that His Father set for Him. The author of the book of Hebrews says, "Consider him." The victory of Jesus over death, hell, and Satan is for us. In the same way, we are called to follow in His steps, turn aside from our former ways of shame, and then live in the shame of the cross just like Jesus did.

Obedience and Surrender Bring Freedom

The shame of the cross is always "surrender" to God's will. "Lord, this doesn't make sense to me but if this is Your will, then I will obey you and follow you." This is what brings us freedom, just as it brought Jesus freedom and great victory. It meant that Jesus, by His obedience to His Father, won all the people of the earth who decide to follow Him back to His Father. In order for Jesus to be victorious, He had to live in the shame of the cross and the boundaries of God's will even though He was God Almighty. It cost Jesus everything, but He considered it nothing in comparison to doing His Father's will.

2 Timothy 1:7–12 (NIV) [7] "For God did not give us a spirit of timidity, but a spirit of power, of love and of self-discipline. [8] So do not be ashamed to testify about our Lord, or be ashamed of me his prisoner. But join with me in suffering for the gospel, by the power of God, [9] who saved us and called us to a holy life—not because of anything we have done but because of his own purpose and grace. This grace was given us in Christ Jesus before the beginning of time, [10] but it has

now been revealed through the appearing of our Savior, Christ Jesus, who has destroyed death and has brought life and immortality to light through the gospel. [11] And of this gospel I was appointed a herald and an apostle and a teacher. [12] That is why I am suffering as I am. Yet I am not ashamed, because I know whom I have believed, and am convinced that he is able to guard what I have entrusted to him for that day."

Paul is telling young Timothy to look to Jesus for his confidence. He has provided everything we need through His life and death and given it to us through His Holy Spirit. This gift involves freedom from our sin and from any shame formally associated with that life of sin. Jesus has turned all our negatives into positives. He has fully prepared us to follow the destiny and purpose for which we have been created. In those boundaries lie freedom, faith, and victory for us to fulfill our calling in God.

The Paradox of Tensions

The Bible is full of numerous paradoxes. Some of these paradoxes have separated Christians over the centuries. For example, issues of faith versus works, issues of ecclesiology, grace versus works, or the place of charismatic gifts and the role of the Holy Spirit. Churches have been divided over these and other tensions that are not clearly agreed upon in Scripture. The very Holy Spirit that we have conflict over is the one who can help enlighten us so we can grasp the paradox of these tensions.

What we need to see is that God has placed these "tensions" in Scripture so that rather than dividing over these issues, we see the two truths in tension. It gives us more understanding than if we just believed one or the other. We like everything to be neat and tidy, but

God is far too majestic and mysterious for us to think we can figure it all out with our little "pea-brains." In humility, we acknowledge that we don't have it all figured out. I expect when I get to heaven I will have some of my pet theories and dogmatic theologies corrected (maybe by the angels).

Many "Calvinists" (those who believe in eternal security), as well as many "Armenians" (those who do not believe in eternal security) will be amazed to discover that they didn't have it all right while on earth. Somewhere between these two positions is more of the truth than they could ever imagine. The reason these two positions exist is because there are Scriptures on both sides of the argument. These tensions need to be "prayed out" (not necessarily worked out) to discover more of God's view. Our human view is so limited. I am writing this as a lifelong "Calvinist" (but one who sees some validity in the Armenian position) who is humbly willing to continually learn more from the Bible; I realize I don't have it all worked out. The more we work out these tensions, the greater becomes our sense of the "full gospel."

How can shame that is in me because of my sin help me stay free from the shame that wants to push me into hiding? It is a paradox. How can that which works against me and traps me be the very thing that provides boundaries for me and keeps me free from more negative shame? It depends on certain choices we make. If we choose to hide in negative shame because hiding is the only way we know how to deal with our shame, then that shame works entirely against us. But if we believe what God's Word says, we can turn negative shame into something that releases goodness to us and releases the protection of God.

The same paradox is referenced in James 4. We must learn to weep before we can know real joy. Psalm 126:5 reminds us that we must first sow in tears before we can reap with songs of joy. The things that have held us captive in negative shame are the things that God uses to give us freedom inside the boundaries of positive shame. Personally, this is what motivates me. I do not want to stand ashamed before Jesus one day, so I choose to live inside His boundaries of right living.

Father, I thank you for Your truth which sets us free. I am grateful that your mysterious truth is far beyond our comprehension and yet You are continually revealing more of Your understanding to us. I am asking You that the truth revealed in this book, however limited it is, would move us toward a greater understanding of Your ways. I want the church of Jesus Christ to walk in freedom to the greatest extent possible on this side of heaven.

I ask that the areas of sin and negative shame that have held Your people captive would be turned into positive shame so that the boundaries of Your Word would continually set Your people free. I ask for this in the mighty and powerful Name of Jesus. Amen.

An Exercise for Your Development

After reading this book, I would encourage you to spend time in quiet prayer telling God exactly where you are at with regard to what you have learned about shame. Are you living in the boundaries that God has set for you? If you feel you have no issues with which to work through, then thank Father God for your previous healing and ongoing protection. If you know you need to work through some of these shame issues, ask the Lord Jesus to help you find a trusted friend or counsellor to help you do that.

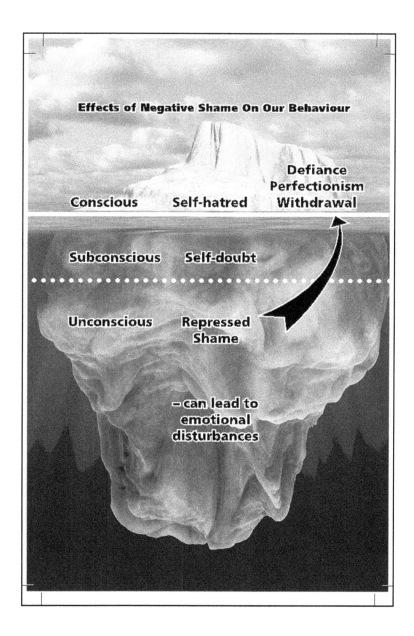

Effects of Negative Shame On Our Behaviour

Defiance
Perfectionism
Conscious   Self-hatred   Withdrawal

Subconscious   Self-doubt

Unconscious   Repressed
Shame

– can lead to
emotional
disturbances

Biblical Understanding of Shame

Definition: Shame is a powerful emotion caused by the awareness of a deficiency in character or behaviour that leaves a person feeling "uncovered"

A feeling of needing to hide something

Shame can function positively
or negatively in a person

Shame used positively

A wholesome attitude that helps define and shape a character of nobility, honour and integrity. Luke 16:3   II Tim. 2:15 "Normal shame" is like breathing air: it's necessary and healthy

Positive shame brings about wholesome changes in people
Psa. 34:5   Jere. 31:19

Increases one's faith and trust in God
Psa. 25:2   II Tim. 1:2

Helps one obey God and keep persevering in obedience
Isa. 50:7   Psa. 119:6

Brings about a repentance and a turning from sin
Ezra 9:6   II Thess. 3:14

God uses shame to bring people to Himself
I Cor. 1:27

Shame used negatively

A conscious or unconscious feeling of self-hatred in one or more areas of life that is like an unhealed wound in the soul
Job 10:15
Unacknowledged shame is destructive. It is like a locked door into the soul

Negative shame blocks the creative potential of one's destiny
Rom. 1:26   Rev. 3:18

Used in a destructive way against ourselves

Used in a destructive way against others

Not having enough shame to repent of sin
Jere. 6:15

People can be shamed into doing things
II Kings 2:17

Lack of shame removes wisdom
Jere. 8:9

Using shame wrongly to bring correction
I Sam. 20:30

Ignoring positive shame brings on more neg. shame
Jere. 13:24-27

Used by God as punishment on His enemies
Jere. 17:13

APPENDIX 3

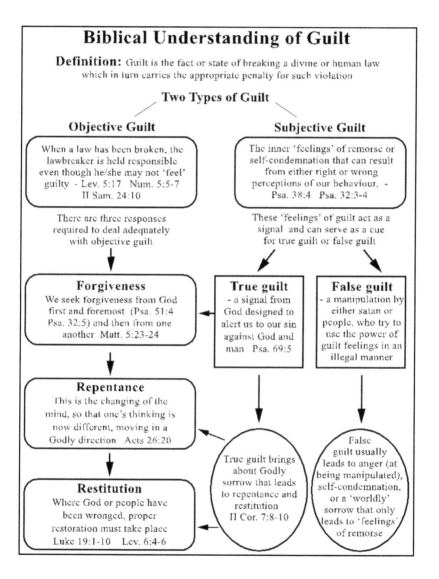

Biblical Understanding of Guilt

Definition: Guilt is the fact or state of breaking a divine or human law which in turn carries the appropriate penalty for such violation

Two Types of Guilt

Objective Guilt

When a law has been broken, the lawbreaker is held responsible even though he/she may not 'feel' guilty - Lev. 5:17 Num. 5:5-7 II Sam. 24:10

There are three responses required to deal adequately with objective guilt

Subjective Guilt

The inner 'feelings' of remorse or self-condemnation that can result from either right or wrong perceptions of our behaviour, - Psa. 38:4 Psa. 32:3-4

These 'feelings' of guilt act as a signal and can serve as a cue for true guilt or false guilt

Forgiveness
We seek forgiveness from God first and foremost (Psa. 51:4 Psa. 32:5) and then from one another Matt. 5:23-24

True guilt
- a signal from God designed to alert us to our sin against God and man Psa. 69:5

False guilt
- a manipulation by either satan or people, who try to use the power of guilt feelings in an illegal manner

Repentance
This is the changing of the mind, so that one's thinking is now different, moving in a Godly direction Acts 26:20

Restitution
Where God or people have been wronged, proper restoration must take place Luke 19:1-10 Lev. 6:4-6

True guilt brings about Godly sorrow that leads to repentance and restitution II Cor. 7:8-10

False guilt usually leads to anger (at being manipulated), self-condemnation, or a 'worldly' sorrow that only leads to 'feelings' of remorse

Characteristics Seen in Adults Who Were Shamed in Childhood

(Check any of the items that are presently characteristic of your behaviour)

- fear of being vulnerable
- fear of sharing one's inner thoughts (in an appropriate context)
- extreme shyness, feelings of inferiority, easily embarrassed
- fear of intimacy and commitment in relationships
- tendency toward *excessive* daydreaming
- patterns of workaholism—using work to prove one has worth and value
- feelings of being unlovable no matter what others tell us
- tendency toward self-centredness and narcissism (removing the shame of rejection by self-love)
- inability to allow one's mistakes to be examined without feelings of defensiveness
- frequent blaming of others as a means of defending ourselves before we can be blamed
- deep sense of loneliness throughout one's life because one feels unworthy of love and thus has a fear of intimacy
- tendency to apologize constantly because shame has closed off the ability to deal with the guilt issues properly
- frequent feelings of anger and judgment toward others in order to shame them before we can be shamed ourselves

- use of excessive makeup or overfocus on clothing to hide perceived flaws in shamed self
- lack of spontaneous expression of normal feelings of joy, fear, anger, sexuality, playfulness, or creativity
- tendency toward perfectionism and performance anxiety because of shame-based personality

CHARACTERISTICS OF
THE POVERTY SPIRIT

A poverty spirit can manifest itself in numerous ways. Here are some:

1) you do not have enough resources for your basic living needs
2) you find a wasting away of the resources you do have
3) you have a constant focus on your lack of provision, even if you have lots
4) you often have a grumbling spirit or a spirit of unthankfulness
5) you manipulate other people to give to you or to notice your plight
6) you have constant fear of not being able to make ends meet
7) you have a lack of generosity in your life and a fear of sharing with others
8) you are often unaware of God's presence and His desire to bless you
9) you fail to tithe consistently and with gladness
10) you have a sense of jealousy or inferiority towards others who have more than you do

CPSIA information can be obtained
at www.ICGtesting.com
Printed in the USA
LVHW042241200319
611330LV00001B/1/P